Diverse Administrators in Peril

Critical Viewpoints
A New Series on Race
Edited by Joe R. Feagin

Upcoming Titles

Mythologizing Black Women: Unveiling White Men's Racist and Sexist Deep Frame, by Brittany C. Slatton

What Don't Kill Us Makes Us Stronger: African American Women and Suicide, by Kamesha Spates

Diverse Administrators in Peril

The New Indentured Class in Higher Education

Edna Chun
and
Alvin Evans

Paradigm Publishers
Boulder • London

Copyright © 2012 Paradigm Publishers

Published in the United States by Paradigm Publishers, 2845 Wilderness Place, Boulder, CO 80301 USA.

Paradigm Publishers is the trade name of Birkenkamp & Company, LLC, Dean Birkenkamp, President and Publisher.

Library of Congress Cataloging-in-Publication Data available from the Library of Congress

Chun, Edna Breinig.
  Diverse administrators in peril : the new indentured class in higher education / Edna Chun and Alvin Evans.
      p. cm. — (New critical viewpoints on society series)
   Includes bibliographical references and index.
   ISBN 978-1-59451-964-2 (hardback : alk. paper) — ISBN 978-1-59451-965-9 (pbk. : alk. paper)
   1. Minority college administrators—United States. 2. Discrimination in higher education—United States. I. Evans, Alvin. II. Title.
   LB2341.C5455 2012
   378.1'11089—dc23

                                                                      2011031842

Printed and bound in the United States of America on acid-free paper that meets the standards of the American National Standard for Permanence of Paper for Printed Library Materials.

Designed and Typeset by Straight Creek Bookmakers.

16 15 14 13 12   1 2 3 4 5

CONTENTS

ACKNOWLEDGMENTS

We dedicate this book to our children—Alexander David Chun, Shomari Evans, Jabari Evans, Kalil Evans, and Rashida VanLeer—as the next generation of leaders who will bring about change. The genesis of this book derives from the challenges we have faced as minority administrators in higher education as well as our strong desire to contribute to the change process. In particular, we believed it to be important to give voice to the experiences of minority, female, and lesbian/gay/bisexual/transgendered administrators who have faced subtle discrimination in their day-to-day work lives, but also to propose solutions that will strengthen their career success and professional contributions.

The administrators in public and private research universities who participated in the survey and interview process conducted for this book provided courageous and honest contributions. Their experiences provide the impetus for systemic, collective efforts to create more inclusive, supportive, and stable administrative working conditions.

Both authors would like to express our gratitude to Professor Joe Feagin, Ella C. McFadden Professor of Sociology at Texas A&M University, for his encouragement and help in the design of this research project as well as his thoughtful suggestions throughout the evolution of the manuscript. We especially thank Dean Birkenkamp, Publisher of Paradigm Books, for his foresight and recognition of the value of this book's contribution to the sociological literature. We also thank Professor Maria Lima of the State University of New York at Geneseo for her insightful review.

Andy Brantley, President and Chief Executive Officer of the College and University Professional Association for Human Resources (CUPA-HR), and Ken Tagawa, Chief Learning Officer of CUPA-HR provided generous support for our work in the development of a contact database of Chief Human Resource Officers for the administrator survey used as the initial basis for the study. Bryan Cook, Director of Policy Analysis, American Council of Education, was especially responsive in supporting our research. We acknowledge with particular gratitude the contributions of Alexander D. Chun in converting the administrator survey into its Web-based format and for his help in the data analysis. And we especially thank Kimberly Thompson for her skilled and responsive research assistance throughout the course of the project.

Alvin Evans wishes to thank President Lester Lefton of Kent State University for his visionary leadership of diversity. President Lefton's actions have been an inspiration to him in doing the research for this book. He would also like to express his deep appreciation to Willis Walker, Esq., Chief Legal Counsel and Vice President for Human Resources, Kent State University, for his keen insights and courage to seek the truth and stand by his convictions. He would like to thank Charlene Reed, Secretary to the Board of Trustees and Chief of Staff, Office of the President, Kent State University, for her generous support. Alvin would also like to acknowledge Reverend Ronald Fowler, Special Assistant to the President, Kent State University, for his incredible source of inspiration and his continued support.

Edna Chun wishes to thank Levi Williams, Esq. and Georgette Sosa Douglass, Esq. for their courageous and visionary leadership in support of diversity as Trustees of Broward College for the last decade. The inspiration that arose amid the secluded rainforest retreat in Mindo, Ecuador on a trip taken by Georgette Sosa Douglass, Edna Chun, and her son, Alexander D. Chun, gave rise to the revision of the scope of our study.

We would like to express special appreciation to our family and friends for their continuous support. Alvin Evans would like to thank Ethel and Horace Bush, Patricia and Leon Scott, Karen and Hassan Rogers, Patricia and Donald Marsh, Brian and Lisa Marshall, Victoria Thomas, and Lesley Green. Edna Chun would like to thank Jay Kyung Chun, David and Laura Tosi Chu, George and Eleanor Chu, Ronnie Rothschild, Winston Thompson, and Karen Williams.

Edna Chun and Alvin Evans

FOREWORD

The United States is a nation of many myths and illusions—political, economic, and demographic. We live by myths carefully taught to us by many of our leaders. Historically, these leaders have virtually all been elite, straight, white men, and today most of our top economic, political, and educational leaders are still elite, straight, white men. They regularly try to tell us, their public, what to think about the most important contours and realities of this society, in regard to its past and present. They are basically conservative, in that they are reluctant to see significant sociocultural changes come to this society. Changes they do allow are usually forced on them by pressures from ordinary Americans and, as the scholar Derrick Bell long ago noted, there is almost always a significant social benefit for elites when they allow major societal changes to happen.

Sadly, such is the case today with the diversification, desegregation, and integration of most major sectors of U.S. society. These were begun under great pressure from once excluded Americans' movements from the early 1900s to the 1960s, but came to significant, if still limited, fruition only when this U.S. elite badly needed to counter the Soviet Union's 1960s influence in dozens of developing countries and also needed people of color to support, as voters and soldiers, the imperialistic warring by the U.S. government in Vietnam.

Since the late 1960s and 1970s, thus, this society has been held up, again at the top by our mostly elite, straight, white, male leaders and their acolytes, as a premier example of a truly diversified and reasonably integrated political and social democracy. However, in fact, we are nowhere near that widely heralded reality. We are, at best, a struggling partial democracy trying to move out from under centuries of oligarchical control by this straight, white, male elite, control exhibited daily in our undemocratic political institutions—for example, in a powerful Senate very disproportionately white, male, and elected on the basis of bounded territories, not on population.

But what about those people of color, those women, those GLBT folks who are often conspicuous in many of our important institutions? Don't they contradict this view of a still oligarchical and straight-white-male-elitist-dominated country? Well, the research data clearly suggest their often modest presence does not fundamentally contradict this view of a continuing elitist oligarchy. For example, the impressive research data from a diverse array of savvy university administrators in this significant book by the courageous researchers and educational administrators, Edna Chun and Alvin Evans, constantly problematize any naïve framing of the United States as a healthily diversified, reasonably well-integrated, and very progressive country on diversity matters. In fact, this rosy framing is a fairy tale often designed to deflect from the country's harsher realities on racial, gender, and GLBT issues.

In this book Chun and Evans go where few educational researchers have dared to tread. There are very few interview studies that touch, in substantial ways, on the everyday lives of black, Hispanic, female, and GLBT administrators at our public and private research universities. This pioneering study tells us much about the everyday administrative and social realities and human and personal costs of being a well-educated, high-achieving American who is not a straight, white man. One would think—and many Americans seem to think that way, according to surveys—that such educational achievement credentials would make for an easily secured American-dream life of general respect and usually untroubled success. Yet, as you will see throughout this book, the forty-three talented administrators surveyed for this book do not report they have achieved this secure American dream. They have not yet seen the proverbial and promised "liberty and justice for all."

Some previous research on black corporate executives by Sharon Collins shows that they often get "ghettoized" and marginalized in non-line staff positions dealing with affirmative action or diversity issues, with a modest scope of authority and little chance to move up to higher corporate managerial levels.[1] Likewise, Chun and Evans report that current national data on top administrative leadership (CFOs and CAOs) in research universities indicate that such leadership is very disproportionately white and male, while administrative positions for diversity efforts are heavily populated by administrators of color.

In their interviews, moreover, Provost Caroline (Chapter 4) makes specific note of the recurring tracking of administrators of color into diversity positions at her university. We also observe in the accounts from their administrative respondents—such as Joan and Therese in Chapter 4 and Lisa in Chapter 5—many insights on the recurring lack of substantial decision-making authority in their administrative positions, such as in regard to scope of authority and important budgeting and staffing. In their survey research, Chun and Evans found that African American administrators rated their decision-making authority, in comparison with the level of their administrative position, as significantly lower than comparable white administrators who were asked that question. Similarly, Hispanic administrators reported their decision-making authority as lower than did their non-Hispanic counterparts.

Moreover, as Chun and Evans demonstrate, these diverse administrators often pay a high price in terms of their personal stress and health for living in the ether of higher administrative levels at important public and private research universities.

Chun and Evans do not just refute reactionary notions that there is no longer racial, gender, and heterosexist discrimination in higher education, for they also provide thoughtful and targeted recommendations for real educational and situational change. Thus, they call for the replacement of administrative accountability regimes that accent a politics of control, centralized power, and market-type management with one that accents instead inclusion, democratic participation, and administrative and personal empowerment.

This major research-oriented book does many important things, but one essential aspect of it is a multifaceted call on all readers to take very seriously the array of career, social, and health implications of continuing overt, subtle, and covert discrimination for diverse administrators and other diverse personnel in our great universities. It is also a call for readers to take very seriously the impact of this discrimination, exclusion, and marginalization on the society generally and on the future of the United States. It is not melodramatic to assert that continuing racism, sexism, and heterosexism significantly endanger the future of the United States. Those facing such quotidian oppression are not the only ones who have paid a high and persisting price. All Americans, indeed all of earth's residents, pay for these kinds of racial, gender, and heterosexist barriers and handicaps. They pay, at a minimum, in the great loss of knowledge to society and to humanity.

Some years ago, the great civil rights leader and NAACP cofounder, W. E. B. Du Bois, spoke out for the broad social benefits of ending large-scale discrimination. The exclusion or marginalizing of Americans of color had long excluded "vast stores" of important knowledge and wisdom.[2] One can extend his insight to the exclusion or marginalizing of women generally and of GLBT Americans. When these diverse Americans are oppressed or marginalized in major institutions, they are *not* the only ones who suffer. Their families and friends certainly suffer. But, in addition, such discrimination against or marginalizing of many people has long meant destroying or excluding much human knowledge and creativity that they hold in their heads and collectively preserved memories. No society can long ignore such a great store of knowledge and ability. By ending racial, gender, and GLBT discrimination we take moral action that is essential for society's long-term social health. In effect, all Americans should benefit from the renewed inclusion of new knowledges and talents in the public and private spheres. And, perhaps most importantly, the democratic ideals held so strongly at a rhetorical and hypothetical level in the United States can have a much better chance of actually becoming reality.

Joe R. Feagin
Texas A&M University

Notes

1. Collins, S. (1996). *Black corporate executives.* Philadelphia: Temple University Press.
2. Du Bois, W. E. B. (1996). On the Ruling of Men. In E. J. Sundquist (Ed.),*The Oxford W. E. B. Du Bois reader,* (pp. 555–557). New York: Oxford University Press.

1

TWENTY-FIRST CENTURY RACISM, SEXISM, AND HETEROSEXISM IN UNIVERSITY ADMINISTRATION

A Primer

> 'Oh, I don't mean you. You're different, you're an Oreo.' ... I said to him, 'You know, I'm sorry I think that most people would recognize that as being a racial slur.' And he says, 'Oh I don't mean that. You are one of them that has common sense.' That was when I asked him to please stop talking because any more compliments from him might really upset me. And so he stopped talking and then after that meeting, a couple of days after that meeting since I was clearly upset about his comments I went and talked to him and used that time as a teachable instant. So I knew I had known for quite some time how he felt about me just because of the color of my skin.
>
> —*Claudia, an African American administrator*

In a so-called post-racial society, Claudia's account of a racialized comment made to her by her supervisor in an open university meeting highlights the continuing presence of white privilege and the prevalence of a white normative structure that penetrates the interactions, practices, understandings, and outcomes within the higher education workplace.

The fragile and unstable working conditions faced by women, minority, and lesbian/gay/bisexual/transgendered (LGBT) administrators in higher education are a little-known and virtually unrecognized reality. This book is devoted to the largely untold story of the impact of twenty-first century forms of subtle discrimination on minority, female, and LGBT administrators at the highest levels within the American research university. As practitioners in the field of higher education, we will explore how discrimination in the higher education workplace has evolved from overt to covert forms of exclusion and marginalization affecting the daily existence of diverse administrators. The subtle yet cumulative nature of contemporary discrimination makes it difficult to pinpoint and even more difficult to litigate, due to the emphasis of existing civil rights legislation upon explicit, overt acts of discrimination.

The collision between everyday life and systems of power in the university workplace is emblematic of larger structural issues within society. Inequality in the workplace is a dynamic, interactive *process*—a process that "reifies existing stratification hierarchies beyond the control of any given individual" (Roscigno, Garcia, and Bobbitt-Zeher, 2007, p. 18). Through the lens of situational analysis, particularly as provided by the first-hand accounts of diverse administrators, we seek to uncover the *process of discrimination* or how everyday life within the academic workplace "is continually eroded, distorted, overpowered by, and subordinated to institutional forces that seem beyond human control" (Burawoy, 1991, p. 1). This process-oriented perspective takes into account not only how dominant group members undertake certain actions (termed "closure") to preserve privilege, but also the efforts of subordinate groups to in some degree resist prevailing stratification efforts ("usurpation") (Roscigno, 2007).

A common assumption on university campuses today is that administrators are a different class—not part of the educational mainstream—an elite group exempt from the difficulties of academia. In fact, personnel actions affecting these employees, particularly terminations, frequently are cloaked in secrecy and rarely make the headlines. Due to the veil of silence and lack of employment protection, diverse administrators can literally disappear from university campuses, almost in Stalinist fashion, just as former Soviet leaders disappeared without a trace from the lineup on the Kremlin wall.

Despite rapid demographic shifts in the United States that will transform this nation into a minority-majority country by 2050, everyday experiences within the leadership environment of the research university still are clouded with the vestiges of racism, sexism, and heterosexism. In the face of the democratizing winds of demographic change both within the United States and in a global society, regressive patterns of subtle discrimination that permeate leadership practices hinder the attainment of progressive and inclusive leadership models needed to advance social change, keep pace with the evolution of knowledge, and mobilize talent to achieve educational outcomes.

The Faculty Perspective

In eras of budget shortages, faculty and labor unions often call attention to the number of university administrators with high salaries and more perquisites than the average faculty member. For example, in March 2009 at the University of Vermont, the faculty union, United Academics, accused the school of being too top heavy, stating it had three vice presidents in 2002 and twenty-two in 2008 (Rathke, 2009). President Daniel Fogel disputed this growth, attributing it to title changes and title creep and indicated that administrator salaries at UVM were below the median of 151 comparable public doctoral research universities. In this regard, the increasing corporatization of American universities is depicted in terms of escalating budgets for managerial and administrative positions with a multiplicity of functions ranging from development, communication, and human resources to information technology, facilities, and security (Glazer-Raymo, 2007). One faculty member in the mythical "Wannabe University" wonders: "Was the focus on education or more efficient management? What about the presence of more and more managerial personnel and the increased centralization of administration, the interminable forms, the emergence of the university as explicitly capitalist institution weighing revenue streams...?" (Tuchman, 2009, p. 4).

While recognizing the opportunity nonacademic positions provide for minorities and women, the rationale for administrative positions has been viewed as in competition with the "heart of the enterprise—faculty, students, academic programs, and scholarship" (Glazer-Raymo, 2007, p. 162). A drift toward "market ethos" is seen by some faculty as the transformation of educational values into business values, including efforts to impose hierarchical organizational models on the faculty (Tuchman, 2009). These models are characterized by an emphasis on efficiency, predictability, calculability, and control (Tuchman, 2009).

Yet frequently commentators are unaware of several factors relating to administrators, particularly in times of economic turmoil. Recent research conducted by Eden King indicates that workplace discrimination can increase in difficult financial times in terms of stigmatization, workplace tension, and the perception of minorities as outsiders (Laskowski, 2009). Negative repercussions can result in layoffs, furlough, fewer promotions, and salary reductions (Laskowski, 2009). Hiring freezes typically affect administrator positions first. In the current economic downturn, research universities have turned to cuts in the administrative and professional ranks first, such as the temporary layoff/furlough program at the University of Northern Iowa ("FY10 Temporary Layoff/furlough Program," 2010), and the layoff of 275 Harvard workers in 2009 (Jan. 2009). These circumstances can leave diverse administrators particularly vulnerable.

Budget cuts have taken their toll on faculty as well, with significant impact on the humanities. Witness the stunning closure of a French department and four other departments at the State University of Albany for "underperformance" (Bauerlein, 2010). Our point is not that administrators have a more difficult time than pre-tenure faculty or even tenured faculty in departments that are eliminated. While the hurdles faced by diverse administrators may be comparable to minority, female, and LGBT pre-tenure faculty, nonetheless, diverse administrators are faced with heightened vulnerability over the course of their entire careers, due to their continuous, year-to-year employment.

Many do not understand the continual balancing act involved in the daily work lives of diverse administrators or the constant barrage of challenges posed by their precarious working conditions. Administrators are usually "at will" employees, typically subject to a single supervisor who may yield almost complete control over the destiny of those they supervise. Unlike faculty whose careers promote individualistic accomplishments solidified through the tenure process, university administrators usually work without employment protection to support the success of the entire institution. As such, rapid turnover of top central administrators can cause faculty to muse about administrators' short tenure and limited power base: "Provosts come and go. Each one brings his own policies. This may just be a temporary policy. *How long do you think we can put off doing what this [provost] wants us to do?*" (Tuchman, 2009, p. 109).

Diverse administrators may be subjected to persistent forms of subtle, covert, and even overt discrimination based upon race, gender, sexual orientation or other factors of difference. For example, a study of 1,054 African American faculty and administrators found that African American men and women experience different realities in higher education, including significant differences in perceptions of inequities and other issues related to campus climate (Singh, Robinson, and Williams-Green, 1995). Although diverse administrators bear the trappings and appearance of power, in some cases the power ascribed to their positions may simply be illusory.

A Tenuous Position

Given the potential for employment discrimination without recourse, diverse administrators can have little more status than twenty-first century "indentured servants." Some may believe that this analogy is exaggerated. But for women, minority, and LGBT administrators employed in the higher echelons of the university and subject to the singular supervision of a powerful individual, the politicized employment atmosphere can create a tenuous professional existence without stability or security.

The concept of indentured servitude refers to individuals whose labor is "bought" and indentured to a specific person, resulting in little, if any, freedom for a specified time period. Indentured servitude arose around 1620 in colonial British America, less than a decade after the initial settlement at Jamestown and persisted until the fourth decade of the nineteenth century (Galenson, 1984). As a central institution of colonial American society, indentured servitude arose to address labor shortages and involved the sacrifice of personal freedom by indentured servants for a period of years to pay off the loan incurred for crossing the Atlantic (Galenson, 1984). In indentured servitude, unlike slavery, the labor of the servant rather than the person was bought and sold (Galenson, 1981). Whereas under slavery, blacks were held in service for life, under indentured servitude in colonial America, whites were bound in service for a limited time period (Galenson, 1981). Typically for a period of four to seven years, indentured servants lived in a state of half-freedom (Cawley, 1999). Following the abolition of slavery and at the height of the transoceanic trade in indentured servitude between 1834 and 1922, more than two million indentured servants were transported overseas from China, India, Africa, Melanesia, and Madeira (Northrup, 1995). As a modified form of exploitation that followed slavery, indentured servitude offered a response to global market demands, providing a competitive and reliable source of inexpensive labor.

To build upon this analogy, diverse administrators often function in an institutional strait jacket, held hostage to their employer by their uncertain status. Unable to speak out without repercussions, they can be subjected to continuous, differential scrutiny, intense pressure, bullying, and even psychological abuse. Few protections exist in the university workplace to mitigate this differential power relationship. Furthermore, the nature of civil rights laws makes discrimination almost impossible to prove, since supervisors are well aware of the need to avoid blatant acts of discrimination.

In the survey conducted for this book, significantly higher levels of mistreatment due to race, $t(18.14)=-2.25$, $p=.037$, were reported by African American and black administrators (M=2.69, SD=1.44) in comparison to white administrators (M=1.69, SD=1.01). In addition, African American and black administrators (M=3.23, SD=1.36) rated their own degree of decision-making authority compared to the level of their position as significantly lower than white administrators asked the same question (M-4.23, SD=.992); $t(37)=2.61$, $p=.013$. Similarly, Hispanic administrators reported their decision-making authority as lower (M=3.00, SD=1.27) than non-Hispanic counterparts (M=4.06, SD=1.15); $t(35)=-2.04$, $p=.049$. In addition, Hispanic administrators indicated that they had to work harder than their peers to prove their worth (M=4.67, SD=.816) in comparison with non-Hispanic administrators (M=2.77, SD=1.36); $t(35)=4.58$, $p=.001$. These statistics reflect the disparate realities faced by diverse administrators that will be discussed in greater depth in later chapters.

Reconceptualizing Leadership

Our purpose in this exploration is to facilitate efforts by universities to create more inclusive work environments that replace top-down, coercive management models with "revolutionary" leadership models focused upon empowerment, inclusiveness, social responsibility, and collaborative management (Kezar and Carducci, 2009). Instead of an accountability regime that incorporates a politics of control, surveillance, centralized power, and market management in the administrative tier (Tuchman, 2009), we propose a new politics that reflects the ideological aims of the academy in terms of inclusion, democratic participation, and empowerment.

We believe that the time is right for change. The "Making Excellence Inclusive" initiative undertaken by the American Association of Colleges and Universities provides a viable framework for inclusion, since it integrates diversity with the fundamental purposes of higher education. Inclusive Excellence focuses upon creating a welcoming community that engages diversity in the service of student and organizational learning and purposively utilizes organizational resources for these ends (Clayton-Pedersen and Musil, 2005).

From this perspective, diversity is a critical, differentiating organizational capability that provides the key to unleashing, mobilizing, and protecting an institution's talent potential in the effort to advance knowledge and sustain innovation (Chun and Evans, 2009). As a result, diversity must be built into the core of higher education where it serves as a "powerful facilitator of institutional mission and societal purpose" (Smith, 2009, p. 3). Due to the challenges of isolation, tokenism, soloing, and differential standards that still face diverse administrators in the university today, this book will introduce approaches designed to shift the dominant authority-based administrative paradigm to one that focuses upon collaboration and empowerment. Such approaches will enhance the work climate, job satisfaction, retention, and career progress of diverse administrators and provide greater synergy with the democratic educational purposes of the university.

We also focus in this book upon ways that individuals facing discriminatory treatment within institutional settings can create counter frames of resistance to oppression. In particular, the liberty-and-justice frame that is articulated in the Declaration of Independence has been a significant counter frame for whites and minorities who have worked to end forms of slavery, Jim Crow, or contemporary discrimination (Feagin, 2010a). A social justice frame or lens provides an alternative perspective that will play a critical role in providing individuals with the ability to take action to reshape institutional practices.

The Paucity of Scholarship

Relatively little scholarship has explored the differential treatment of minorities, women, and LGBT individuals within the administrative ranks of the research university. Jackson and O'Callaghan provide an assessment of the representation of academic leaders in colleges and universities with an emphasis on faculty pipeline issues and faculty demographic data as well as student affairs administrators using two national datasets (Jackson and O'Callaghan, 2009a). A small body of literature examines the experiences of minority and female administrators, particularly at high levels such as president or chancellor (see for example Harvey, 1999; Holmes, 2003; Jones, 2001) as well as the perils faced by minority change agents in leadership roles (see Valverde, 2003). A number of insightful studies have examined the challenges for African American administrators (see for example Jackson, 2002; Jackson, 2003; Jackson, 2004; Jackson and Flowers, 2003; Singh, Robinson, and Williams-Green, 1995) and barriers to the success of women administrators (see for example Mitchell, 1993; Nidiffer and Bashaw, 2001; Sagaria, 2007).

These analyses represent, however, only the tip of the scholarly iceberg. The body of work on administrators remains sparse and varied and will require amplification to extend qualitative research on the personal experiences of diverse administrators (Jackson and O'Callaghan, 2009a). Little can be found on the first-person experiences of diverse administrators since it is far more difficult for university professionals to share their experiences than for tenured faculty, due to fear of retaliation and lack of job security. This book seeks to amplify the small body of existing research by probing more deeply into the work experiences of minority, female, and LGBT administrators. Our goal is to assist institutions of higher education in the creation of more inclusive and equitable working environments that promote the leadership talents and creative contributions of diverse administrators.

Investigative Variables

This book will examine how the fragile employment conditions of women, minority, and LGBT administrators can create career instability that heightens stress and exacts a significant psychological and physiological toll on those in the administrative ranks. Due to the fact that presidents have distinctly different challenges and responsibilities in overseeing institutions and reporting through boards of trustees, they are not included in this study.

Selection of the doctoral research university for this study provides a common basis for examining the role of administrators within institutions of similar scope, size, resource base, research focus, and reliance upon a workforce of tenure track and tenured full-time faculty. The 277 research universities in the United States represent 6 percent of the total of 4,485 higher education institutions. Research universities are large, complex organizations enrolling thousands of students and involving expenditures of hundreds of millions or even billions of dollars, and requiring an array of significant administrative decisions (Duderstadt, 2001). In fiscal year 2008, for example, twenty research universities accounted for 30 percent of federal research academic spending (Britt, 2009). Furthermore, most research universities must file affirmative action plans as recipients of $50,000 or more in federal contracts. This dependence upon federal funding has heightened the focus of research universities upon programs seeking to eliminate discrimination (Glazer-Raymo, 2007).

The definition of administrator derives from the legal guideline provided by the Fair Labor Standards Act (FLSA). Administrators are individuals whose assignments involve managing a department, subdivision, or institution and whose primary work relates to policies or general business operations and requires discretion and judgment (U.S. Department of Education, 2003).

Research indicates that organizational inequality for women and minorities increases in both magnitude and intensity as individuals ascend the organizational pyramid (Elliott and Smith, 2004; Wright and Baxter, 2000). Similarly, the glass ceiling effect refers to gender or racial differences not explicable by other job-related characteristics that are greater at higher levels than lower levels of the organization, limit advancement, and increase over time during the course of a career (Cotter, Hermsen, Ovadia, and Vanneman, 2001; Jackson and O'Callaghan, 2009b). As a result, we specifically seek to explore and document the work experiences of higher level minority, female, and LGBT administrators with significant responsibilities for institutional oversight. Although universities employ different definitions of director, we have used the benchmark title of director as a threshold for this study, since it denotes positions with a substantial scope of responsibility often accompanied by supervisory and budgetary authority. Through an examination of the perils of "at will" employment for diverse administrators at higher levels in the university, we hope to begin to unmask the invisible and unmarked landscape that affects career success, retention, and advancement.

The focus upon the specific attributes of race, gender, and sexual orientation in this book is based upon the prominence and salience of these attributes in historical patterns and practices of discrimination in the United States. In terms of race and gender in particular, physical identifiability and discrimination operate in mutually reinforcing patterns within American society (Aguirre and Turner, 1998). Employees with invisible stigma such as gay/lesbian, bisexual, and transgendered individuals must determine whether to disclose their identity, a dilemma that causes "disclosure disconnects" resulting in psychological stress and inner conflict (Ragins, 2008). In this regard, a study of 534 members of national gay rights organizations found perceived workplace discrimination to be significantly related to the degree of disclosure of sexual orientation (Ragins and Cornwell, 2001). The stigma associated with a group that has been the subject of social persecution and devaluation affects disclosure decisions, which take place along a continuum in differing life settings (Creed, 2006; King, Reilly, and Hebl, 2008; Ragins, 2008). Transgendered individuals, whose gender expression is perceived to violate social norms of male and female identity, have experienced hate crimes at higher rates than lesbian, gay, and bisexual individuals and at a rate comparable to anti-Moslem violence since 2002 (Sánchez and Vilain, 2009; Stotzer, 2007).

Furthermore, within the workplace, historically disadvantaged groups have systematically faced oppression, resulting in patterns of discrimination that take place in forms of inequity (Prasad, Pringle, and Konrad, 2006; Smith, 2009). Institutional isms such as racism, sexism, and heterosexism have a disparate impact on targeted groups, limit access and success of individuals or groups who would otherwise be successful, and are unrelated to institutional purpose or mission (Smith, 2009).

Diversity in University Administration—Myth or Reality?

Diverse administrators are only beginning to break the glass ceiling in America's 277 research universities. Table 1.1 reflects the overall growth rate of 42 percent in full-time administrator positions at research universities between 1997 and 2007. The patterns of employment also reveal a 67 percent increase in women administrators and an 89 percent increase in the number of minority administrators during this time period. Percentage gains by African American, Asian American, and Hispanic female administrators were roughly double those attained by their male counterparts.

Nonetheless, Department of Education statistics aggregate all levels of administrator into one single measure and do not depict minority or female progress to higher administrative levels. Women tend to be clustered in lower-level leadership positions with minority women holding a smaller percentage of the available positions (Berryman-Fink, Lemaster, and Nelson, 2003; Konrad and Pfeffer, 1991; McCurtis, Jackson, and O'Callahan, 2009). Since

Table 1.1 Change in Administrators by Race at Research Universities Between Fall 1997 and Fall 2007

	1997	% of Total	2007	% of Total	Numerical Change	% of Change
Nonresident Alien	182	0.3	581	0.7	399	219.7
Black non-Hispanic	4,813	7.9	7,539	8.8	2,726	56.6
American Indian/ Alaska Native	220	0.4	330	0.4	110	50
Asian or Pacific Islander	1,277	2.1	2,902	3.4	1,625	127.3
Hispanic	1,605	2.6	4,188	4.9	2,583	160.9
White non-Hispanic	52,464	86.4	69,294	80.5	16,830	32.1
Race/ethnicity unknown	157	0.3	1,277	1.5	1,120	713.4

US Department of Education, 1997, 2007.

senior academic officers are the typical pathway to the presidency, less than 10 percent of chief academic officers are minorities, and women represent only 23 percent of incumbents in senior academic roles (King and Gomez, 2008). These statistics provide a benchmark for the future composition of the university presidency in terms of the pool of eligible candidates (Jackson, 2004). Furthermore, the data indicates that leadership and decision making in the research university mirror the racial stratification of our society. As social theorist Joe Feagin points out, "We still live in a very hierarchical society in racial, class, and gender terms, one where white men continue to make the lion's share of major decisions about our economic development, laws, and major public policies" (Feagin, 2010b, p. 193).

Attainment of structural representation is an essential first step in addressing the participation of diverse administrators. It is a necessary but not sufficient condition in the journey toward genuine inclusion. Such representation is needed to create a critical mass of women and minorities within the administrative ranks. For example, a study of 821 colleges and universities involving 11,412 positions found that the percentage of women or minorities in a job title and in the organization coupled with the presence of a woman or minority previously in a given position were statistical predictors of hiring for women and minorities (Konrad and Pfeffer, 1991).

Research indicates that critical mass is an important threshold linked to the psychological climate for diverse administrators at work, since subjective perceptions of token status can lead to overall perceptions of inequity (King, Hebl, George, and Matusik, 2010). Tokenism theory suggests that underrepresentation is a primary cause of negative work experiences for minorities (King, Hebl, George, and Matusik, 2010; Yoder, 1991). Individuals who function as tokens are more visible, leading to increased performance pressures, social isolation, and stereotyping (King, Hebl, George, and Matusik, 2010).

The rapid forces of globalization have fostered a growing emphasis on talent, innovation, and creativity, demanding transformation of university cultures to be more inclusive (Chun and Evans, 2009). In the context of the changing demographics of student populations, universities have recognized the value of diversity in the educational experience, as articulated in the 2003 Supreme Court decisions relating to admissions at University of Michigan (*Grutter v. Bollinger,* 539 U.S. 306 and *Gratz v. Bollinger*). In a representative bureaucracy, decisions made by leadership groups need to address the concerns of constituents (Jackson and O'Callaghan, 2009a). From a student and faculty perspective, diverse administrators play an important role in warming the chilly climate, promoting the well-being and satisfaction of diverse faculty particularly those who are new and untenured, and in enhancing the academic success of minority students (Harris and Nettles, 1996; Jackson, 2002; Jackson and O'Callaghan, 2009a).

We begin the discussion in this chapter by examining the typical employment conditions of administrators and the clear differentiation between the academic and nonacademic tracks. We then discuss the conceptual framework of systemic institutional discrimination as well as how twenty-first century subtle discrimination occurs within the administrative domain. As a key feature of this discussion, we examine the disconnection of the current management prototype from the democratic mission and purposes of the university. The chapter concludes with a brief discussion of the limited legal avenues available to administrators in counteracting subtle discrimination.

Two Tracks: The Academic and Nonacademic Administrator

Due to their lack of protection by unions, civil service requirements, or tenure, administrators at higher levels in the educational hierarchy usually serve at the pleasure of their supervisor or the president. In fact, many employment letters state this fact in simple terms. Higher ranking administrators typically report directly to an executive-level position such as a provost, vice president, or the president.

The track of academic administrators such as deans, assistant and associate deans, associate provosts, provosts, and in some institutions, department chairs, differs significantly from nonacademic administrators. Academic administrators frequently have retreat rights to the faculty, providing protection in a tenured teaching line. Academic administrators usually must possess a terminal degree as well as substantive academic experience, since they act on promotion, tenure, merit, and other academic policy matters.

For nonacademic administrators, a more corporate/bureaucratic model of management applies (Chesler, Lewis, and Crowfoot, 2005). They operate without tenure in areas such as student affairs, human resources, finance, information technology, and facilities. Their positions typically require at least master's degree preparation in a variety of fields as well as experience in administration.

Unlike faculty and similar to professional managers in corporate settings, both administrator tracks are governed by unwritten rules: loyalty to one's boss, refraining from speaking out of turn or engaging in public criticism of the administration or one's superiors, and maintaining the corporate dress code (Tuchman, 2009). And new administrators hired from national labor pools tend to be perceived by the faculty as "outsiders," strangers who can leave tomorrow—corporate creatures on a rest stop in their career history (Tuchman, 2009).

Two examples highlight the fragile employment conditions of diverse administrators in predominantly white research universities and the potentially different consequences between the academic and nonacademic track. Both examples illustrate how budget cutting and reorganization can serve as rationales for dire employment actions as well as the precipitous and even dehumanizing nature of these actions due to a lack of administrative safeguards. In both cases the firing of individuals whose direct responsibilities were the protection of equity and diversity for the university has considerable irony.

The following examples also underscore the ghettoization and racialization of affirmative action and equity positions within the university—a similar trend noted by Sharon Collins among black corporate executives in Chicago through comparative interviews undertaken in 1986 and 1992 (Collins, 1997). Of the seventy-six executives interviewed, fifty-one had held affirmative action positions (Collins, 1997). Such positions typically have high ranking titles, are highly visible, but have little power and often serve as a "race-related mobility trap for black managers" (Collins, 1997, p. 82).

In 2004 Dr. Ed Richardson, a former Auburn University board member assumed the interim presidency of Auburn. The Southern Association of Colleges and Schools (SACS) had just placed Auburn University on probation for lack of transparency in board decision-making processes, failure of the president to control the athletics program, and the tendency to promote interim staff into permanent positions (Gerber, 2005). Richardson immediately embarked on a reorganization that involved the dismissal of fourteen administrators and coaches including Janet Saunders, executive director for affirmative action and equal employment opportunity, a black female administrator with twenty years of experience in affirmative action, consolidating her duties into the Human Resources Department (University Business Staff, 2004).

A letter from the Auburn University Association of University Professors identified a chilling atmosphere in which employees were fired during their lunch hour (Editor, Communications and Marketing), had their email privileges removed before they could return to the office (Vice President of Alumni Affairs), and were told they could not pick up their things in the office unless escorted (E.E.O.C. officer) (Executive Committee, 2004). Willie Larkin, Auburn's first black Faculty Senate Chair, questioned Richardson's sensitivity to minorities like Saunders, noting that "the firings have affected morale. Everyone wonders if they will be next" (Stripling and Nix, 2004). An atmosphere of friction continued among faculty and the administration during Richardson's tenure, despite Auburn's removal from academic probation by the Southern Association of Colleges and Schools (Olliff, 2010).

As a second example, on November 6, 2009, the *Washington Post* reported that several hundred students marched to the administration building at the University of Maryland to protest the firing of Dr. Cordell Black, associate provost for equity and diversity, in one of the largest protests since the Vietnam War era (De Vise, 2009). Dr. Black, an African American, holds a Ph.D. in seventeenth-century French Literature from the University of Michigan, and had held the position for eighteen years. With the announcement that the diversity position would become part-time, the University Provost, Dr. Nariman Farvardin, indicated that the change was for budgetary reasons. However, Dr. Black's removal would save the university only $10,000, since he was returning to a tenured faculty line. Some described the furor over Black's removal as reflecting deeper tensions relating to a lack of transparency in decision making (Walker, 2010). Despite the difficult circumstances involved, Dr. Black's continued ability to speak out about the situation while still at the university derives from his ability to retreat to a tenured faculty line (Black, 2010).

These cases illustrate the perilous employment status of diverse university administrators as well as the abrupt character of administrative actions undertaken with or without any articulated reasons. Restructuring can occur like a thunderclap (Tuchman, 2009). Such actions underscore the dispensable nature of administrators and the fragility of their circumstances. In precarious situations that can occur with little warning, diverse administrators walk a continuous tightrope that exacts a significant toll upon their psychological and physical resources.

The professional and personal price for the affected individuals cannot be underestimated. Workplace discrimination emanates to the affected individual's life and home environment (Feagin and McKinney, 2003). It has a demonstrated effect on self-esteem when those impacted by discrimination internalize contemporary forms of oppression and unconsciously become their own oppressors through self-blame and inappropriate attribution of instances of everyday discrimination to their own personal or dispositional inadequacies (Crocker, Voelkl, Testa, and Major, 1991; Evans and Chun, 2007; Hardiman and Jackson, 1997).

Dimensions of the Administrative Playing Field

While the purposes of the university are democratic in the quest for truth and in support of academic freedom, the existing hierarchical administrative model does not support the full realization of these principles. The emergence of the administrator class over the last half century has created a management track with its own distinct challenges that has, to date, failed to incorporate the democratic traditions that embody the core of the educational mission. By contrast, contemporary scholarship conceptualizes a model of leadership that moves away from authority-based, hierarchical frameworks to increasingly democratic forms of leadership that focus on process and values (Kezar and Carducci, 2009). Revolutionary leadership assumptions affected by the civil rights and feminist movements of the 1960s and 1970s and the rise of globalization have replaced the emphasis on coercion and control with empowerment, cross-cultural understanding, collaboration, complexity, and social responsibility (Kezar and Carducci, 2009).

During the period between the twentieth- and twenty-first centuries, the university evolved dramatically in terms of its intellectual, social, and professional role without a corresponding change in its organization, governance, and management (Rhodes, 2001). As slow-moving institutions that are resistant to change, universities have relied upon static, hierarchical organizational structures in contrast to the principles of high-performing organizations committed to unleashing the creative potential of staff and focused upon engagement (Alfred and Rosevear, 2000). Furthermore, the glacial pace of the university in its decision-making and academic change processes may not be responsive enough to allow it to control its own destiny, as the tidal wave of social forces transforms higher education in unforeseen ways (Duderstadt, 2001).

Within the higher education enterprise itself, educators appear to have lost the language connecting the purposes of higher education to democracy in the retreat from core American values of equal access, opportunity, equality, and autonomy to an emphasis upon competitive market advantage and job training (Giroux and Giroux, 2004). The values of respect, decency, and compassion and the ability to recognize antidemocratic forms of power are not part of the vocabulary of the market (Giroux and Giroux, 2004). The rhetoric of democracy is challenged every day by the extent of inequity and its persistence in many domains (Smith, 2009). In addition to the heritage of democracy, academic freedom is the legitimizing concept of the academic enterprise that establishes a zone of protection and self-regulation surrounding teaching and inquiry related to the purposes of academic inquiry (Menand, 1996). Yet this delicate zone of freedom represents unknown territory for administrators, who operate at the other end of the spectrum, in a high-penalty zone without protections.

The academic institution suffers from disconnection: decisions and actions at one level in the organization are isolated from decisions and actions at other levels, resulting in a breakdown in shared meaning about organizational life (Levin, 2000). Furthermore, disparate cultures create conflicts among constituent groups that accelerate the tendency toward multiple goals, competing centers of power, and vulnerability to external forces (Chesler, Lewis, and Crowfoot, 2005). The struggle is not only over authority and control, but also over definition and identity (Levin, 2000). As a result, the bureaucratic model of administration with its emphasis on elite management, authoritarian control of subordinates, and orthodoxy of fundamental values (Chesler, Lewis, and Crowfoot, 2005) is at variance with the faculty model of autonomy, academic rigor, and functional independence.

The view that higher education is exempt from discriminatory practices and that barriers arising from race, gender, and sexual orientation have disappeared is at variance with the historical record. Denial of the existence of discrimination as a lingering problem in American education is disproved by a long history of discriminatory practices that included legalized segregation persisting as late as the 1950s (Feagin, Vera, and Imani, 1996). Racial barriers remain commonplace on predominantly white college campuses and represent manifestations of socially organized practices that deny minorities dignity, opportunities, time, positions, and rewards available to white Americans (Feagin, Vera, and Imani, 1996). And higher education has historically promoted both the symbolic and material interests of white elites who have used positions of power to legitimize privilege at the expense of minority groups (Chesler, Lewis, and Crowfoot, 2005).

Women faculty leaders have led the way in chronicling the persistence of discrimination within higher education, probably due to not only their scholarly background but also the protected status that tenure provides (see for example Cooper and Stevens, 2002; Glazer-Raymo, 2008; Smith, 2009; Smith and Wolf-Wendel, 2005; Stanley, 2006). The strenuous process of attaining tenure has attracted significant scholarly attention for its differential impact on women and minorities. The time-delimited pressure cooker of tenure attainment in the highly charged and intense atmosphere of university environments has commonalities with the continual and unrelenting pressure faced by diverse administrators over the course of their careers.

Furthermore, the *intersection* of multiple jeopardies of race, gender, and sexual orientation compounds and exacerbates the issues of exclusion for minority, female, and LGBT individuals. While racism, sexism, and heterosexism are not the same, they coalesce in interlocking forms of oppression that take shape in both visible and deeply embedded and invisible ways (McIntosh, 1988). Minority women in higher education, for example, face double jeopardy or a unique type of *ethgender* discrimination that requires them to be smarter, work harder, and be more articulate than everyone else to overcome the sexism and racism they face in the workplace (Carter, Pearson, and Shavlik, 1996; King, 2005).

Simultaneous membership in multiple oppressed groups and the accompanying psychological stress suggests overlap and at least partial fusion of the constructs of racism and sexism in everyday experience (King, 2005, Reid and Comas-Diaz, 1990). Racism may intensify the impact of sexism and vice versa, making the whole of individual oppression greater than the sum of its parts (Reid and Comas-Diaz, 1990). The "double" or "triple" minority status faced by some LGBT individuals compounds the decision to "come out," as these individuals face stigmatization and juggle the sometimes conflicting membership in multiple identity groups (Greene, 1994; Harper and Schneider, 2003).

While examining the impact of sustained patterns of subtle discrimination on the career success of women, minority, and LGBT administrators, we must also explore the organizational framework and institutional culture that permit such practices to persist within the university environment.

The Structural Framework for Discriminatory Practices

In order to understand how subtle discriminatory practices take shape within the higher education workplace, we must first unpack the structural dimensions of oppression to see how the complex substrata of exclusionary interconnections, networks, and processes permeate institutional life. Scholars have posited that institutional discrimination is *systemic* and the result of deeply imbedded, and often invisible forms of discrimination and cumulative patterns of interpersonal discrimination (Bonilla-Silva, 2009; Feagin, 2006; Feagin, 2010a; Karlsen and Nazroo, 2004). The source of systemic discrimination arises from socially based discrimination that is replicated within the culture, norms, and practices of an institution (Feagin, 2006; Meyer, 2003). Systemic racism takes place through dominance and hierarchical interaction and "is centrally about the creation, development, and maintenance of white privilege, economic wealth, and sociopolitical power over four centuries" (Feagin, 2010a, p. 14).

Joe Feagin's *Racist America: Roots, Current Realities, and Future Reparations* (2010a) provides the most current overview of the racialized United States including how discrimination transpires within everyday practice in institutional settings. Specifically, he notes that "... the majority of whites who do the serious discriminating in this society are those with significant power to bring harm, such as white employers ..." (p. 141). White executives responsible for hiring and promotions maintain conventional stereotypes that affect their willingness to promote diverse employees and often make use of overtly marginalizing looks and language that expresses their discomfort (Feagin, 2010a).

The legacy of systemic discrimination must be placed within historical context. Prior to the last civil rights legislation that ended legal segregation, for more than 85 percent of American history in the 350 years between 1619 and 1969, our country was grounded in legal segregation and extensive slavery (Feagin, 2010b). Systemic discrimination continues to exist due to the continuing benefits and material advantages it offers to the dominant class (Bonilla-Silva, 2003). It perpetuates white privilege: the invisible knapsack of privileges, special assets, and advantages that reflect how unearned power is conferred systematically (McIntosh, n.d.). And similarly, male privilege and heterosexual privilege preserve the material advantages offered to the dominant group in power.

Systemic discrimination is composed of five main components: 1) attitudes; 2) emotions; 3) ideology; 4) practices; and 5) institutions (McKinney and Feagin, 2003). Eight generic dimensions capture the channels in which institutional discrimination is transmitted within higher education: mission, culture, power, membership, social relations and climate, technology, resources, and boundary management (Chesler, Lewis, and Crowfoot, 2005). These interdependent dimensions reinforce one another to influence organizational behavior such as when the *culture* fosters disrespect of minorities, when *power* does not deliver on the commitment to justice, when diverse *membership* in campus communities is not solicited, when the *technology* of how unfinished materials are converted to finished products in the curriculum does not reflect diversity, and when *boundaries* limit community interface and reinforce discriminatory practices (Chesler, Lewis, and Crowfoot, 2005).

The dynamics of power govern the work environment for diverse administrators since the disadvantages faced by historically excluded and disenfranchised groups affects their organizational experiences (Prasad, Pringle, and Konrad, 2006). A lack of power is the central feature of minority group status (Loue and Sajatovic, 2009). As one educator writes, the social view of white, male, and European as the "right" race and sex in American society translates in the workplace to situations that capitalize on the attributes of power and privilege, creating a hostile work environment for women and minorities (Myers, 2002). Sexual minorities similarly are invisible and unacknowledged by institutions, but when acknowledged and visible are problematized as abnormal and unnatural (Herek, Gillis, and Cogan, 2009).

Forms of institutional discrimination take shape through two avenues: individually mediated discrimination and organizational forms of discrimination. In other words, individual bias, attitudes, and beliefs as well as the application of organizational processes and procedures reinforce the practice of discrimination (Griffin, 1991; Sidanius and Pratto, 1999). Individual behaviors are the vehicle for the process of marginalization. These behaviors activate the underlying hierarchical power relations in which whites reenact patterns of oppression (Feagin, 2010a).

Individually mediated discrimination can result in the instrumental use of organizational processes to create subjective and unfairly low performance assessments that devalue work and efforts and influence the outcomes of compensation, reappointment, and promotion (Einarsen and Skogstad, 1996; Pettigrew and Martin, 1987; Winkler, 2000). These processes offer the opportunity for subjective and differential interpretation, through the subtleties of language and application of differential standards. By rhetorical and semantic moves that disguise hidden discrimination, the appearance of neutrality and objectivity is maintained (Bonilla-Silva, 2009). The interplay between individually mediated discrimination and organizational discrimination can create a powerful and virtually inextricable employment web for the diverse administrator.

The suave and seemingly nonracial phenomenon of color-blind racism has emerged in recent years to justify arrangements and practices that sustain white privilege (Bonilla-Silva, 2009). Color-blind racism is a slippery yet powerful ideology that disguises discriminatory views through a virtually impregnable wall that employs four predominant frames: 1) abstract liberalism that adopts the language of liberalism yet justifies existing exclusionary practices; 2) naturalization or the notion that racial phenomena such as segregation are natural; 3) cultural racism that defends the status quo through cultural arguments; and 4) minimization of racism (Bonilla-Silva, 2009). "Race-neutral" and "color-blind" policies and strategies must be scrutinized closely to determine whether such strategies sustain white privilege or the unearned advantages of being white (Smith, 2009).

Real or Imaginary? Identifying Forms of Subtle, Everyday Discrimination

One of the distinct difficulties with subtle forms of twenty-first century discrimination is that these types of discrimination are cloaked, disguised, and difficult to pinpoint. Exclusionary practices take place along a continuum of attitudes and actions, rather than representing sheer oppositional categories like "racist" or "not racist" (Trepagnier, 2007). Subtle forms of everyday, twenty-first century discrimination occur within organizational settings through micro-aggressions and micro-inequities. A growing body of scholarship has identified the cumulative nature of micro-incursions or micro-inequities that create everyday discrimination within the workplace and, in turn, heighten job stress and reduce job satisfaction (see for example Deitch et al., 2003; Rowe, 2008; Smith, Yosso, and Solorzano, 2006; Solorzano, Ceja, and Yosso, 2000; Sue, 2010; Sue et al., 2007; Young, 2003). In 1973 Mary Rowe, Ombudsperson at the Massachusetts Institute of Technology, began to write about these ephemeral, difficult-to-prove events that have a cumulative and corrosive effect, concluding that micro-inequities have been a "principal scaffolding for discrimination in the U.S." (Rowe, 2008, p. 2).

Micro-inequities represent recurring patterns of devaluing messages, behavior, and conduct that impair and discourage performance and can damage self-esteem and cause withdrawal (Young, 2001). Each person who is a recipient of micro-inequities is an expert on what constitutes a micro-inequity in a given situation: such barriers can include not inviting African Americans to strategy meetings, leaving women out when field trips are taken, blaming problems on those who are different, and expecting failure from the individual of difference (Rowe, 2008). Micro-inequities represent an unpredictable, intermittent type of "negative reinforcement," an irrational form of "punishment" that occurs in context of merit, but without relevance to performance (Rowe, 2008).

Research on micro-aggressions and micro-inequities illuminates how forms of everyday discrimination can isolate, marginalize, and exclude diverse individuals in the workplace. These brief, commonplace, daily indignities communicate hostile, derogatory, or negative slights toward individuals due to their group membership and have monumental impact (Sue et al., 2007; Rowe, 2008; Sue, 2010; Young, 2006). Micro-inequities can take place through facial expressions, hand gestures, choice of words, eye contact, and tone of voice, and reveal what is behind the masks that connect myths of incompetence with race, gender, and other factors (Young, 2006).

A taxonomy of micro-aggressions identifies three major forms of such inequities: 1) *micro-assaults* including name-calling, avoidant behavior, and more overt forms of discrimination; 2) *micro-insults* such as rude and insensitive behavior that demeans others; and 3) *micro-invalidation* through communications that nullify or minimize the experiential reality of targets (Sue, 2010; Sue et al., 2007). Micro-aggressions occur both through verbal and nonverbal mini-assaults and may involve layered insults based on multiple identities such as race, gender, class, and sexual orientation (Smith, Yosso, and Solorzano, 2006). Some common themes with hidden messages include: ascription of intelligence (statements like "You are a credit to your race"); second-class citizenship (statements like "Where are you really from" and "If you don't like it here, go back to your country"); and use of sexist/heterosexist language (statements labeling assertive women as "bitches") (Sue, 2010). Recall how Christine's supervisor called her an "Oreo" at the opening of the book, implying she was an exception to her race. In later chapters, we shall see further evidence of the cumulative impact of micro-aggressions that undermine professional competence, credibility, and success in the interview narratives conducted for this study.

For diverse administrators, the texture and patterns of everyday life in the university workplace can be threaded with daily micro-incursions that undermine their contributions and create a double standard for their achievements. Our survey findings reveal that African American/black administrators believe to a greater degree that minority employees experience covert discrimination on a frequent basis ((M=3.92, SD=.862) than do white participants (M=3.04, SD=1.248); $t(37)=-2.289$, $p=.028$.

Micro-incursions directed at diverse others arise swiftly and sometimes unconsciously through forms of "unintentional intolerance" that are hardwired as stereotypes into a person's consciousness (Robbins, 2007). Such reactions can be triggered within a couple of seconds or in a "blink" (Gladwell, 2005). For example, in the Implicit Association Test (IAT), individuals form impressions within as little as 400 and 600 milliseconds, as a series of black and white faces appear on the screen (Gladwell, 2005). Analysis of more than 2.5 million IATs from three datasets gathered over six years indicates that approximately 68 percent of participants paired black skin with bad and white skin with good (Nosek et al., 2007).

Micro-aggressions occur both through commission and omission. For example, Karen Schmaling writes of experiences with gender micro-aggressions as a female dean when she walks by the President and Engineering Dean (both male) who are talking about the round of golf they played with donors (Schmaling, 2007). She muses, "Wow—that's more time in one day than I have spent with the President in total. I don't play golf so I couldn't do that if I wanted to. I don't know of any interests I share with the President" (Schmaling, 2007, p. 16).

Once hired, diverse administrators must face an invisible gauntlet of formalized processes and organizational barriers that determine how their performance is evaluated, how compensation is allocated, and the continuation of employment. These practices vary, depending on institutional policy and practice. But since the determination of outcomes may depend on a single powerful individual, forms of recourse are, at best, extremely limited.

Behavioral barriers range from avoidance, distancing, and lack to support, to the application of differential standards as well as failure to empower and include in decision making (Evans and Chun, 2007). Stereotyping, aggressive communication, and the myth of incompetence and underperformance all serve to undermine the success of women, minorities, and LGBT administrators (Evans and Chun, 2007; Holder-Winfield, 2007). Minority administrators, in particular, can be caught in the same battle minority faculty face of constantly having to prove their competence. If the administrator maintains the status quo without creating major new initiatives, he/she can be viewed as not accomplishing enough; on the other hand, if he/she leads significant new initiatives, the administrator can be perceived as instigating too much change.

A key aspect of marginalization and oppression is the "misrecognition" of the full humanity and experiences of diverse individuals, underscoring the concept of invisibility identified by Ralph Ellison in his famous *Invisible Man* (1995). As Ellison (1995) writes, "You ache with the need to convince yourself that you do exist in the real world, that you're a part of all the sound and anguish, and you strike out with your fists, you curse and you swear to make them recognize you. And, alas, it's seldom successful" (p. 4).

Diverse individuals are both visible as a member of the group they represent and invisible as individuals (Smith, 2009). Visibility involves heightened attention directed toward tokens within their workgroups coupled with "exacerbated pressures to perform" (Yoder, 1994, p. 150). In this regard, a minority faculty member writes of the paradox of wiping out the most visible aspect of one's bodily presence as follows (Laubscher, 2006):

> After four years serving on faculty and university committees together, walking past each other in the hallways, and brushing shoulders in the faculty dining room, I have been introduced to the head of a department on the same floor as mine no less than four times, each time with him saying (the biggest, friendliest smile on his face), 'I don't believe we've met. Which department are you in?' (p. 202)

The term *behavioral asymmetry* identifies how the behavioral repertoires of individuals contribute to the reinforcement of group-based hierarchical relationships (Sidanius and Pratto, 1999). Forms of behavioral asymmetry from supervisor to employee can embody prevailing stereotypes, psychological biases, and even the imposition of forms of psychological abuse (Sidanius and Pratto, 1999).

Institutional culture is the medium for transmitting, reinforcing, and perpetuating forms of covert discrimination. Within the context of prevailing norms, assumptions, and cultural beliefs, university culture can support existing practices by ignoring and dismissing forms of subtle discrimination as imaginary and nonexistent. In this regard, three kinds of pressures have been identified within institutional culture: *normative pressures* that arise from the socialization of institutional members into interpretations and beliefs; *coercive pressures* resulting from external regulation and other internal forces; and *mimetic pressures* that copy existing patterns and perpetuate them (Leicht and Fennell, 2008). All of these pressures work in concert to create an environment ranging from unintentional intolerance and a state of denial to active support for maintenance of subterranean discriminatory practices.

The Gap between Civil Rights Legislation and Sophisticated Discrimination

The clear legal watershed of Title VII of the Civil Rights Act (1964) established the litmus test for proving overt discrimination. Yet with the passage of time over the past half century, a covert and institutionalized system of veiled discrimination has replaced overt and brutal forms of racial oppression in the pre-civil rights era (Bonilla-Silva, 2009). As a result, the level of sophistication regarding discriminatory practices has increased and perpetrators seldom engage in overt acts that could be proved to be discriminatory. The bar needed to prove discrimination under existing laws is extremely high and usually requires clear evidence of blatant or outright discrimination.

Specifically, the doctrinal framework of Title VII requires the plaintiff in a disparate treatment case to prove that the employer was motivated by discriminatory racial or other animus at the exact time an adverse employment action was taken whereas in a disparate impact case the plaintiff has to establish how a neutral policy has a disparate impact on protected class members (Lee, 2005). The proper role for an unconscious bias or subtle discrimination case remains an open question as a theory of liability and element of proof in employment litigation (Lee, 2005; Neuhauser, 2008). Courts have acknowledged the existence of unconscious bias for some time and have more recently begun to engage in explicit discussion of its prevalence and its inclusion in Title VII's prohibitions in several decisions (Lee, 2005). Yet proving subtle discrimination is still a significant legal challenge offering considerable hurdles.

Typically, administrators serve "at will" or with, at best, limited term contracts. As a result, they can be dismissed without cause. Even having above-average performance evaluations and substantive evidence of contributions to the institution does not provide a guarantee of continued employment. Unless they have acquired faculty retreat rights and serve in academic administrative appointments, administrators are typically only eligible for a limited period of severance (three to six months) in cases of involuntary separation.

As at will employees, the only protective course of action for minority, female, and LGBT administrators facing employment actions that include termination would be to prove discriminatory treatment under federal or state statutes. Federal statutes prohibiting discriminatory practices include Title VII of the Civil Rights Act, the Equal Pay Act of 1963, the Age Discrimination in Employment Act of 1967 (ADEA), Title I of the Americans with Disabilities Act of 1990 (ADA), and most recently the Genetic Information

Nondiscrimination Act of 2008 (GINA). Almost half the states and the District of Columbia have protective statutes that prohibit sexual orientation discrimination in public and private employment. Issues of LGBT rights, however, remain a subject of intense debate and can be viewed as barriers to legal protections against sexual orientation discrimination (Levitt et al., 2009).

Other courses of legal recourse include protection from retaliation under Title VII of the Civil Rights Law of 1964 or from retaliation from reporting or refusing to engage in illegal acts under the Whistleblower Enhancement Act of 2007 or state whistleblower acts. Another avenue for legal action is to file a claim of retaliation such as when an individual has filed a complaint of discrimination and then suffers an adverse action affecting job assignments, promotions, layoff, termination, performance evaluations, and any other term or condition of employment. In some cases, retaliation may be a more viable legal approach. Claims of retaliation can be based upon threats, unjustified negative references, and increased surveillance ("Facts about Retaliation," n.d.). Yet administrators may be afraid to file claims for fear of jeopardizing their positions and creating a negative relationship with their supervisor.

A number of studies have examined how a climate of organizational justice contributes to employee perceptions of equity in workplace decisions. Organizational justice is the psychology of justice within organizational settings that hinges on perceptions of fairness and influences employee performance, behaviors, and outcomes (Fortin, 2008). It consists of four key dimensions: 1) distributive justice or the perceived fairness of outcomes; 2) procedural justice or the fairness of process leading to outcomes; 3) interpersonal or interactional justice or the quality of respect, sensitivity, truthfulness, and personal treatment that accompany everyday encounters and formal decision making; and 4) informational justice or the amount and quality of information shared during processes (Fortin, 2008).

In this regard, a study of fifty-four district units of a large Fortune 500 company with an average of 4,702 employees per unit found that a stronger climate of procedural justice was linked to lower filing of lawsuits following EEOC claims (Wallace, Edwards, Mondore, and Finch, 2008). Similarly, a study of 996 recently fired or laid-off employees in central Ohio found that a significant determinant of filing suit for wrongful termination was the way employees were treated. Between one in seven and one in five of those who felt they had been dismissed without dignity, lied to, or treated unfairly filed suit (Brockner, 2006; Lind, Greenberg, Scott, and Welchans, 2000). Women and minorities filed at higher rates based on perceptions of poor treatment rather than the perceived likelihood of winning or ease of access to attorneys (Lind, Greenberg, Scott, and Welchans, 2000). Furthermore, a study of 220 marketing managers revealed that pay fairness predicted both job satisfaction and organizational commitment (Deconinck and Bachmann, 2007). Job satisfaction and organizational commitment are variables directly related to turnover (Deconinck and Bachmann, 2007).

Since an atmosphere of procedural justice is shaped by management, the focus of the organization must be upon the interpersonal and moral conduct of managers who enact decisions and implement policies (Bies and Tyler, 1993). Practices of equity and diversity are essential to the creation of an inclusive community that reflects principles of social and organizational justice. As institutions struggle to attain and retain a critical mass of diverse administrators, they must pay attention to the importance of a supportive climate that incorporates diversity into a shared culture that promotes caring, trust, and teamwork (Wolf-Wendel, 2000).

Concluding Perspectives

In the university today, minority, female, and LGBT administrators still face significant hurdles that preclude their career success. The burden of systemic, institutional patterns of racism, sexism, and heterosexism coupled with individuated forms of conscious or unconscious bias can foster adverse employment conditions that heighten the potential for mistreatment. The lack of employment protection for administrators creates a tenuous professional existence at best. In the continual challenge to prove themselves and their competence, diverse administrators may encounter daily challenges in the form of micro-inequities that severely tax psychological and personal resources. Patterns of subtle discrimination that occur on an everyday basis may not be readily discernible to outside observers, create ambiguity for the targets, and elude legal remedies due to the emphasis of civil rights laws on acts of overt discrimination. The cumulative effect of patterns of subtle discrimination can erode self-confidence, reduce job satisfaction, and impact the retention of diverse administrators.

Furthermore, a hierarchical model of administration that emphasizes control at the expense of participation, collaboration, and empowerment fails to draw upon the creative resources and talent potential available to the university. Such a model can allow the interjection of subjectivity and personal preference in formal organizational processes affecting compensation, advancement, and retention. The contradiction between the university's meritocratic ideology and differences in treatment based on ascriptive characteristics remains a source of substantive organizational problems (Prasad, Pringle, and Konrad, 2006). This contradiction fundamentally undermines the principles of democratic participation represented in contemporary leadership models and reflected in the university's mission and aspirations.

While the analogy of "indentured servitude" may seem extreme, it clearly conveys the notion of how contemporary employment conditions can hold diverse administrators hostage without stability or security. In the effort to attain Inclusive Excellence within the university, new approaches to leadership will help transform administrative culture to promote the full participation and empowerment of all its members. In this era of globalization, the university needs to draw upon the rich and diverse talents of its workforce to optimize its organizational capabilities as it seeks to contribute to the expansion of knowledge in a rapidly changing, global, multi-cultural society. The challenge is to create a multivocal culture, in which creativity and differences flourish (Tierney, 2008).

In the next chapter, we shall explore the impact of discrimination and stress upon health outcomes to understand the effect of discriminatory work climates on health, well-being, and job satisfaction. We will also examine how diverse administrators construct frames of resistance in terms of concrete career strategies, psychological approaches, and social alliances.

Works Cited

Aguirre, A., and Turner, J. (1998). *American ethnicity: The dynamics and consequences of discrimination* (2nd ed.). New York: McGraw-Hill.

Alfred, R., and Rosevear, S. (2000). Organizational structure, management, and leadership for the future. In A. M. Hoffman and R. W. Summers (Eds.), *Managing colleges and universities: Issues for leadership* (pp. 1–28). Westport, CT: Bergin and Garvey.

Bauerlein, M. (2010, December 10). *Guest post by Scott Sprenger: In the humanities, how should we define 'decline'.* Message posted to http://chronicle.com/blogs/brainstorm.

Berryman-Fink, C., Lemaster, B. J., and Nelson, K. A. (2003). The women's leadership program: A case study. *Liberal Education,* 89(1), 59–63.

Bies, R. J., and Tyler, T. R. (1993). The "litigation mentality" in organizations: A test of alternative psychological explanations. *Organization Science,* 4(3), 352–366.

Black, C. (2010), *Part two of Dr Cordell Black's speech*. Retrieved March 8, 2010, from http://www.youtube.com/watch?v=Q5qT9EIxJRk.

Bonilla-Silva, E. (2003). *Racism without racists: Color-blind racism and the persistence of racial inequality in the United States*. Lanham, MD: Rowman and Littlefield.

Bonilla-Silva, E. (2009). *Racism without racists: Color-blind racism and the persistence of racial inequality in the United* State (3rd ed.). Lanham, MD: Rowman and Littlefield.

Britt, R. (2009). *Federal government is largest source of university R&D funding in S&E; Share drops in FY 2008*. Retrieved March 9, 2010, from http://www.nsf.gov/statistics/infbrief/nsf09318/nsf09318.pdf.

Brockner, J. (2006). Why it's so hard to be fair. *Harvard Business Review,* 84(3), 122–129.

Burawoy, M. (1991). Introduction. In M. Burawoy, A. Burton, A. A. Ferguson, and K. J. Fox (Eds.), *Ethnography unbound: Power and resistance in the modern metropolis* (pp. 1–7). Berkeley, CA: University of California Press.

Carter, D., Pearson, C., and Shavlik, D. (1996). Double jeopardy: Women of color in higher education. In C. Turner, M. Garcia, A. Nora, and L. I. Rendon (Eds.), *Racial and ethnic diversity in higher education* (pp. 460–464). Needham Heights, MA: Simon and Schuster Custom.

Cawley, A. S. (1999). A passionate affair: The master-servant relationship in seventeenth-century Maryland. *Historian,* 61(4), 751–763.

Chesler, M. A., Lewis, A., and Crowfoot, J. (2005). *Challenging racism in higher education: Promoting justice*. Lanham, MD: Rowman and Littlefield.

Chun, E., and Evans, A. (2009). *Bridging the diversity divide: Globalization and reciprocal empowerment in higher education* (ASHE-ERIC Higher Education Reports, Vol. 35, No. 1). San Francisco: Jossey-Bass.

Clayton-Pedersen, A., and Musil, C. M. (2005). *Introduction to the series*. Retrieved May 15, 2011, from http://www.aacu.org/inclusive_excellence/documents/ Williams_et_al.pdf.

Collins, S. M. (1997). *Black corporate executives: The making and breaking of a black middle class*. Philadelphia, PA: Temple University Press.

Cooper, J., and Stevens, D. D. (Eds.). (2002). *Tenure in the sacred grove: Issues and strategies for women and minority faculty*. Albany: State University of New York Press.

Cotter, D. A., Hermsen, J. M., Ovadia, S., and Vanneman, R. (2001). The glass ceiling effect. *Social Forces,* 80(2), 655–681.

Creed, W. E. D. (2006). Seven conversations about the same thing: Homophobia and heterosexism in the workplace. In A. M. Konrad, P. Prasad, and J. K. Pringle (Eds.), *Handbook of workplace diversity* (pp. 371–400). Thousand Oaks, CA: Sage Publications.

Crocker, J., Voelkl, K., Testa, M., and Major, B. (1991). Social stigma: The affective consequences of attributional ambiguity. *Journal of Personality and Social Psychology,* 60(2), 218–228.

De Vise, D. (2009). *U-Md. Students protest official's firing*. Retrieved March 8, 2010, from http://www.washingtonpost.com/wp-dyn/content/article/2009/11/05/AR2009110502997.html.

Deconinck, J., and Bachmann, D. (2007). The impact of equity sensitivity and pay fairness on marketing managers' job satisfaction, organizational commitment and turnover intentions. *Marketing Management Journal,* 17(2), 134–141.

Deitch, E. A., Barsky, A., Butz, R. M., Chan, S., Brief, A. P., and Bradley, J. C. (2003). Subtle yet significant: The existence and impact of everyday racial discrimination in the workplace. *Human Relations,* 56(11), 1299–1324.

Duderstadt, J. J. (2001). Fire, ready, aim! University decision-making during an era of rapid change. In W. Z. Hirsch and L. E. Weber (Eds.), *Governance in higher education: The university in a state of flux* (pp. 26–51). Paris: Economica.

Einarsen, S., and Skogstad, A. (1996). Bullying at work: Epidemiological findings in public and private organizations. *European Journal of Work & Organizational Psychology,* 5(2), 185–201.

Elliott, J. R., and Smith, R. A. (2004). Race, gender, and workplace power. *American Sociological Review,* 69(3), 365–386.

Ellison, R. (1995). *Invisible man* (2nd ed.). New York: Random House.

Evans, A., and Chun, E. B. (2007). *Are the walls really down? Behavioral and organizational barriers to faculty and staff diversity* (ASHE-ERIC Higher Education Reports, Vol. 33, No. 1). San Francisco: Jossey-Bass.

Executive Committee. (2004). *Letter from AU AAUP to SACS regarding Auburn University.* Retrieved March 10, 2010, from http://www.auburn.edu/academic/societies/aaup/final_sacs_letter.htm.

Facts about retaliation. (n.d.). Retrieved March 13, 2010, from http://www.eeoc.gov/laws/types/facts-retal.cfm.

Feagin, J. R. (2006). *Systemic racism: A theory of oppression.* New York: Routledge.

Feagin, J. R. (2010a). *Racist America: Roots, current realities, and future reparations* (2nd ed.). New York: Routledge.

Feagin, J. R. (2010b). *The white racial frame: Centuries of racial framing and counter-framing.* New York: Routledge.

Feagin, J. R., and McKinney, K. D. (2003). *The many costs of racism.* Lanham, MD: Rowman and Littlefield.

Feagin, J. R., Vera, H., and Imani, N. (1996). *The agony of education: Black students at white colleges and universities.* London: Routledge.

Fortin, M. (2008). Perspectives on organizational justice: Concept clarification, social context integration, time and links with morality. *International Journal of Management Reviews,* 10(2), 93–126.

FY10 temporary layoff/furlough program: Academic administrators, institutional officials, merit supervisory & confidential, and professional & scientific employees. (2010). Retrieved March 20, 2010, from http://www.vpaf.uni.edu/hrs/documents/uni_fy10_temp_layoff_info.pdf.

Galenson, D. W. (1981). The market evaluation of human capital: The case of indentured servitude. *The Journal of Political Economy,* 89(3), 446–467.

Galenson, D. W. (1984). The rise and fall of indentured servitude in the Americas: An economic analysis. *The Journal of Economic History,* 44(1), 1–26.

Gerber, L. G. (2005). *Auburn University: A case study in the need for sunshine.* Retrieved

March 11, 2010, from http://www.aaup.org/AAUP/pubsres/academe/2005/MJ/ Feat/gerb.htm.

Giroux, H. A., and Giroux, S. S. (2004). *Take back higher education: Race, youth, and the crisis of democracy in the post-civil rights era.* New York: Palgrave Macmillan.

Gladwell, M. (2005). *Blink: The power of thinking without thinking.* New York: Little, Brown and Company.

Glazer-Raymo, J. (2007). Gender equality in the American research university: Renewing the agenda for women's rights. In M. A. D. Sagaria (Ed.), *Women, universities, and change: Gender equality in the European Union and the United States* (pp. 161–178). New York: Palgrave Macmillan.

Glazer-Raymo, J. (2008). *Unfinished agendas: New and continuing gender challenges in higher education.* Baltimore, MD: Johns Hopkins University Press.

Greene, B. (1994). Ethnic-minority lesbians and gay men: Mental health and treatment issues. *Journal of Consulting and Clinical Psychology,* 62(2), 243–251.

Griffin, J. T. (1991). Racism and humiliation in the African American community. *The Journal of Primary Prevention,* 12(2), 149–167.

Hardiman, R., and Jackson, B. W. (1997). Conceptual foundation for social justice courses. In M. Adams, L. A. Bell, and P. Griffin (Eds.), *Teaching for diversity and social justice: A sourcebook* (pp. 16–29). New York: Routledge.

Harper, G. W., and Schneider, M. (2003). Oppression and discrimination among lesbian, gay, bisexual, and transgendered people and communities: A challenge for community psychology. *American Journal of Community Psychology,* 31(3–4), 243–252.

Harris, S. M., and Nettles, M. T. (1996). Ensuring campus climates that embrace diversity. In L. I. Rendon and R. O. Hope (Eds.), *Educating a new majority: Transforming America's educational system for diversity* (pp. 330–371). San Francisco: Jossey-Bass.

Harvey, W. B. (Ed.). (1999). *Grass roots and glass ceilings: African American administrators in predominantly white colleges and universities.* Albany: State University of New York Press.

Herek, G. M., Gillis, J. R., and Cogan, J. C. (2009). Internalized stigma among sexual minority adults: Insights from a social psychological perspective. *Journal of Counseling Psychology,* 56(1), 32–43.

Holder-Winfield, N. (2007). *Recruiting and retaining a diverse workforce.* Portland, OR: First Books.

Holmes, S. L. (2003). Black female administrators speak out: Narratives on race and gender in higher education. *National Association of Student Affairs Professionals Journal,* 6(1), 45–65.

Jackson, J. F. L. (2002). Retention of African American administrators at predominantly white institutions: Using professional growth factors to inform the discussion. *College and University,* 78(2), 11–16.

Jackson, J. F. L. (2003). Toward administrative diversity: An analysis of the African American male educational pipeline. *The Journal of Men's Studies,* 12(1), 43–60.

Jackson, J. F. L. (2004). Engaging, retaining, and advancing African Americans in executive-level positions: A descriptive and trend analysis of academic administrators in higher and postsecondary education. *The Journal of Negro Education,* 73(1), 4–20.

Jackson, J. F. L., and Flowers, L. A. (2003). Retaining African American student affairs administrators: Voices from the field. *College Student Affairs Journal,* 22(2), 125–136.

Jackson, J. F. L., and O'Callaghan, E. M. (2009a). *Ethnic and racial administrative diversity: Understanding work life realities and experiences in higher education* (ASHE-ERIC Higher Education Reports, Vol. 35, No. 3). San Francisco: Jossey-Bass.

Jackson, J. F. L., and O'Callaghan, E. M. (2009b). What do we know about glass ceiling effects? A taxonomy and critical review to inform higher education research. *Research in Higher Education,* 50(5), 460–482.

Jan, T. (2009, June 24). Harvard workers stunned by layoffs: Endowment loss cited; 275 jobs cut. *The Boston Globe.* Retrieved March 20, 2010, from http://www .boston.com/news/local/massachusetts/articles/2009/06/24/harvard_workers _stunned_by_layoffs_of_275/.

Jones, L. (Ed.). (2001). *Retaining African Americans in higher education: Challenging paradigms for retaining students, faculty & administrators.* Sterling, VA: Stylus.

Karlsen, S., and Nazroo, J. Y. (2004). Fear of racism and health. *Journal of Epidemiology and Community Health,* 58. Retrieved March 21, 2010, from http://jech.bmj.com/ content/58/12/1017.extract.

Kezar, A., and Carducci, R. (2009). Revolutionizing leadership development: Lessons from research and theory. In A. Kezar (Ed.), *Rethinking leadership in a complex, multicultural, and global environment: New concepts and models for higher education* (pp. 1–38). Sterling, VA: Stylus.

King, E. B., Hebl, M. R., George, J. M., and Matusik, S. F. (2010). Understanding tokenism: Antecedents and consequences of a psychological climate of gender inequity. *Journal of Management,* 36(2), 482–510.

King, E. B., Reilly, C., and Hebl, M. (2008). The best of times, the worst of times: Exploring dual perspectives of "coming out" in the workplace. *Group & Organization Management,* 33(5), 566–601.

King, J., and Gomez, G. G. (2008). *On the pathway to the presidency: Characteristics of higher education's senior leadership.* Washington, DC: American Council on Education.

King, K. R. (2005). Why is discrimination stressful? The mediating role of cognitive appraisal. *Cultural Diversity and Ethnic Minority Psychology,* 11(3), 202–212.

Konrad, A. M., and Pfeffer, J. (1991). Understanding the hiring of women and minorities in educational institutions. *Sociology of Education,* 64(3), 141–157.

Laskowski, T. (2009). *New research shows that workplace discrimination increases in times of economic turmoil.* Retrieved March 21, 2010, from http://eagle.gmu.edu/ newsroom/741/.

Laubscher, L. (2006). Color in the interstice, or, what color, this faculty of color? In C. A. Stanley (Ed.), *Faculty of color: Teaching in predominantly white colleges and universities* (pp. 196–215). Bolton, MA: Anker Publishing Company.

Lee, A. J. (2005). *Unconscious bias theory in employment discrimination litigation.* Retrieved March 15, 2010, from http://www.law.harvard.edu/students/orgs/crcl/vol40_2/lee .pdf.

Leicht, K. T., and Fennell, M. L. (2008). Who staffs the US leaning tower? Organizational change and diversity. *Equal Opportunities International,* 27(1), 88–106.

Levitt, H. M., Ovrebo, E., Anderson-Cleveland, M. B., Leone, C., Jeong, J. Y., Arm, J. R., et al. (2009). Balancing dangers: GLBT experience in a time of anti-GLBT legislation. *Journal of Counseling Psychology,* 56(1), 67–81.

Levin, J. S. (2000). The Practitioner's dilemma: Understanding and managing change in the academic institution. In A. M. Hoffman and R. W. Summers (Eds.), *Managing colleges and universities: Issues for leadership* (pp. 29–42). Westport, CT: Bergin and Garvey.

Lind, E. A., Greenberg, J., Scott, K. S., and Welchans, T. D. (2000). The winding road from employee to complainant: Situational and psychological determinants of wrongful-termination claims. *Administrative Science Quarterly,* 45(3), 557–590.

Loue, S., and Sajatovic, M. (Eds.). (2009). *Determinants of minority mental health and wellness.* New York: Springer.

McCurtis, B. R., Jackson, J. F. L., and O'Callahan, E. M. (2009). Developing leaders of color in higher education: Can contemporary programs address historical employment trends?. In A. Kezar (Ed.), *Rethinking leadership in a complex, multicultural, and global environment: New concepts and models for higher education* (pp. 65–92). Sterling, VA: Stylus.

McIntosh, P. (1988). *White privilege and male privilege: A personal account of coming to see correspondences through work in women's studies.* Retrieved March 13, 2010, from http://www.iub.edu/~tchsotl/part2/McIntosh%20White%20Privilege.pdf.

McIntosh, P. (n.d.). *White privilege: Unpacking the invisible knapsack.* Retrieved January 21, 2009, from http://www.powervote.org/files/White%20Privilege.pdf.

McKinney, K., and Feagin, J. R. (2003). Diverse perspectives on doing antiracism: The younger generation. In A. W. Doane and E. Bonilla-Silva (Eds.), *White out: The continuing significance of racism* (pp. 233–252). New York: Routledge.

Menand, L. (1996). The limits of academic freedom. In L. Menand (Ed.), *The future of academic freedom* (pp. 3–20). Chicago: University of Chicago Press.

Meyer, I. H. (2003). Prejudice, social stress, and mental health in lesbian, gay, and bisexual populations. *Psychological Bulletin,* 129(5), 674–697.

Mitchell, P. T. (Ed.). (1993). *Cracking the wall: Women in higher education administration.* Washington, DC: College and University Personnel Association.

Myers, L. W. (2002). *A broken silence: Voices of African American women in the academy.* Westport, CT: Bergin and Garvey.

Neuhauser, M. (2008). *Avoiding liability for unconscious bias and subtle discrimination.* Retrieved March 13, 2010, from http://www.ebglaw.com/showarticle.

Nidiffer, J., and Bashaw, C. T. (2001). *Women administrators in higher education: Historical and contemporary perspectives.* Albany: State University of New York Press.

Northrup, D. (1995). *Indentured labor in the age of imperialism, 1834–1922.* New York: Cambridge University Press.

Nosek, B. A., Smyth, F. L., Hansen, J. J., Devos, T., Lindner, N. M., Ranganath, K. A., et al. (2007). Pervasiveness and correlates of implicit attitudes and stereotypes. *European Review of Social Psychology,* 18, 36–88.

Olliff, M. T. (2010). *Auburn University (AU).* Retrieved March 11, 2010, from http://www.encyclopediaofalabama.org/face/Article.jsp?id=h-1649.

Pettigrew, T. F., and Martin, J. (1987). Shaping the organizational context for black American inclusion. *Journal of Social Issues, 43*(1), 41–78.

Prasad, P., Pringle, J. K., and Konrad, A. M. (2006). Examining the contours of workplace diversity: Concepts, contexts and challenges. In A. M. Konrad, P. Prasad, and J. K. Pringle (Eds.), *Handbook of workplace diversity* (pp. 1–22). Thousand Oaks, CA: Sage Publications.

Ragins, B. R. (2008). Disclosure disconnects: Antecedents and consequences of disclosing invisible stigmas across life domains. *Academy of Management Review, 33*(1), 194–215.

Ragins, B. R., and Cornwell, J. M. (2001). Pink triangles: Antecedents and consequences of perceived workplace discrimination against gay and lesbian employees. *Journal of Applied Psychology, 86*(6), 1244–1261.

Rathke, L. (2009). *Union critical of UVM administrator salaries.* Retrieved March 20, 2010, from http://www.unitedstaff.us/2009/03/14/union-critical-of-uvm -administrator-salaries/.

Reid, P. T., and Comas-Diaz, L. (1990). Gender and ethnicity: Perspectives on dual status. *Sex Roles, 22*(7/8), 397–408.

Rhodes, F. H. T. (2001). The university at the millennium: Missions and responsibilities of research universities. In W. Z. Hirsch and L. E. Weber (Eds.), *Governance in higher education: The university in a state of flux* (pp. 3–14). Paris: Economica.

Robbins, S. L. (2007). *Teachable moments: Short stories to spark diversity dialogue.* Otsego, MI: PageFree Publishing.

Roscigno, V. J. (2007). *The face of discrimination: How race and gender impact work and home lives.* Lanham, MD: Rowman and Littlefield.

Roscigno, V. J., Garcia, L. M., and Bobbitt-Zeher, D. (2007). Social closure and processes of race/sex employment discrimination. *The Annals of the American Academy of Political and Social Science, 609*(1), 16–48.

Rowe, M. (2008). *Micro-affirmations & micro-inequities.* Retrieved March 15, 2010, from http://web.mit.edu/ombud/publications/micro-affirm-ineq.pdf.

Sagaria, M. A. D. (2007). *Women, universities, and change: Gender equality in the European Union and the United States.* New York: Palgrave Macmillan.

Sánchez, F. J., and Vilain, E. (2009). Collective self-esteem as a coping resource for male-to-female transsexuals. *Journal of Counseling Psychology, 56*(1), 202–209.

Schmaling, K. B. (2007). *Gender micro-aggressions in higher education: Proposed taxonomy and change through cognitive-behavioral strategies.* Retrieved April 21, 2010, from http://www.forumonpublicpolicy.com/archivesum07/schmaling.pdf.

Sidanius, J., and Pratto, F. (1999). *Social dominance: An intergroup theory of social hierarchy and oppression.* New York: Cambridge University Press.

Singh, K., Robinson, A., and Williams-Green, J. (1995). Differences in perceptions of African American women and men faculty and administrators. *The Journal of Negro Education, 64*(4), 401–408.

Smith, D. G. (2009). *Diversity's promise for higher education: Making it work.* Baltimore, MD: Johns Hopkins University Press.

Smith, D. G., and Wolf-Wendel, L. (2005). *The challenge of diversity: Involvement or alienation in the academy?* (ASHE-ERIC Higher Education Reports, Vol. 31, No. 1) (Rev. ed.). San Francisco: Jossey-Bass.

Smith, W. A., Yosso, T. J., and Solorzano, D. G. (2006). Challenging racial battle fatigue on historically white campuses: A critical race examination of race-related stress. In C. A. Stanley (Ed.), *Faculty of color: Teaching in predominantly white colleges and universities* (pp. 299–327). Bolton, MA: Anker Publishing Company.

Solorzano, D., Ceja, M., and Yosso, T. (2000). Critical race theory, racial micro-aggressions, and campus racial climate: The experiences of African American college students. *The Journal of Negro Education,* 69(1/2), 60–73.

Stanley, C. A. (Ed.). (2006). *Faculty of color: Teaching in predominantly white colleges and universities.* Bolton, MA: Anker Publishing Company.

Stripling, J., and Nix, J. (2004). *What's next for Auburn?* Retrieved March 10, 2010, from http://www.ewa.org/docs/Stripling.doc.

Stotzer, R. (2007). *Comparison of hate crime rates across protected and unprotected groups.* Retrieved September 3, 2010, from The University of California Los Angeles, Williams Institute Web site: http://www.centeronhalsted.org/programs/Williams_Institutes_Hate_Crimes_Report.pdf.

Sue, D. W. (2010). *Micro-aggressions in everyday life: Race, gender, and sexual orientation.* Hoboken, NJ: John Wiley and Sons.

Sue, D. W., Capodilupo, C. M., Torino, G. C., Bucceri, J. M., Holder, A. M. B., Nadal, K. L., et al. (2007). Racial micro-aggressions in everyday life: Implications for clinical practice. *American Psychologist,* 62(4), 271–286.

Tierney, W. G. (2008). *The impact of culture on organizational decision-making: Theory and practice in higher education.* Sterling, VA: Stylus.

Trepagnier, B. (2007). *Silent racism: How well-meaning white people perpetuate the racial divide.* Boulder, CO: Paradigm Publishers.

Tuchman, G. (2009). *Wannabe U: Inside the corporate university.* Chicago: University of Chicago Press.

University Business Staff. (2004). *Auburn's reorganization interim president fires staff.* Retrieved March 10, 2010, from http://www.aaup.org/AAUP/pubsres/academe/2005/MJ/Feat/gerb.htm.

U.S. Department of Education, National Center for Education Statistics, Integrated Postsecondary Education System (IPEDS). (2003). *Fall 2003 public research universities faculty types by race.*

Valverde, L. A. (2003). *Leaders of color in higher education: Unrecognized triumphs in harsh institutions.* Walnut Creek, CA: AltaMira Press.

Walker, C. (2010). *Budget cuts at college park create unrest.* Retrieved March 8, 2010, from http://mobile.baltimoresun.com/inf/infomo?view=top_stories_item&feed:a=balt_sun_1min&feed:c=topstories&feed:i=51385247&nopaging=1.

Wallace, J. C., Edwards, B. D., Mondore, S. P., and Finch, D. M. (2008). Employee discrimination claims and employee-initiated lawsuits: Does procedural justice climate moderate the claims-disputes relationship? *Journal of Managerial Issues,* 20(3), 313–326.

Winkler, J. A. (2000). Faculty reappointment, tenure, and promotion: Barriers for women. *The Professional Geographer,* 52(4), 737–750.

Wolf-Wendel, L. E. (2000). Women-friendly campuses: What five institutions are doing right. *The Review of Higher Education,* 23(3), 319–345.

Wright, E. O., and Baxter, J. (2000). The glass ceiling hypothesis: A reply to critics. *Gender & Society,* 14(6), 814–821.

Yoder, J. D. (1991). Rethinking tokenism: Looking beyond numbers. *Gender & Society,* 5(2), 178–192.

Yoder, J. D. (1994). Looking beyond numbers: The effects of gender status, job prestige, and occupational gender-typing on tokenism processes. *Social Psychology Quarterly,* 57(2), 150–159.

Young, S. (2001). *Micro-inequities: The power of small.* Retrieved March 16, 2010, from http://www.insighteducationsystems.com/PDF/ProfilesinDivSummer2001.pdf.

Young, S. (2003). *Micro-inequities: The power of small.* Retrieved March 17, 2010, from http://www.insighteducationsystems.com/PDF/WorkforceDiversity2003.pdf.

Young, S. (2006). *Micromessaging: Why great leadership is beyond words.* New York: McGraw-Hill.

2

THE INTERPLAY BETWEEN DISCRIMINATION, STRESS, AND HEALTH OUTCOMES

> Then it dawned upon me with a certain suddenness that I was differ-
> ent from the others; or like, mayhap, in heart and life and longing, but
> shut out from their world by a vast veil.... It is a peculiar sensation, this
> double-consciousness, this sense of always looking at one's self through
> the eyes of others, of measuring one's soul by the tape of a world that
> looks on in amused contempt and pity. One ever feels his two-ness,—an
> American, a Negro; two souls, two thoughts, two unreconciled strivings;
> two warring ideals in one dark body, whose dogged strength alone keeps
> it from being torn asunder.
>
> —*W. E. B. Du Bois,* The Souls of Black Folk,
> *1903 [2003], pp. 8–9*

What are the daily processes, experiences, and behaviors that make the administrative playing field qualitatively different for diverse administrators?
Lisa, an African American administrator in an elite research institution
interviewed for this study, describes her own day-to-day state of uncertainty,
looking for clues as to whether her role is being taken seriously. As part of
the dilemma of attributional ambiguity in which minorities and women are
uncertain whether or not to attribute certain actions to discrimination, Lisa
must continually try to determine if things that occur happen to others in
the same way. As she explains:

You know, even in my position ... I am not sure if I'm really, if they are taking seriously what I need to do here or that my job, my position is taken that seriously. I don't know that. I have got to feel my way around until I get some clues either pro or con. And I'm an African American female. We do that every day, feeling around for pro's and con's. Does that happen to some other people? I'm sure it does, but not to the rate that we are doing it. Trying to feel our way around. Is this an important position? Is it a real position? Is the outreach to me true and genuine or are they trying to fill a slot in their Affirmative Action plan until they get someone they really want? The interesting thing and I wish more people would say it out loud, Affirmative Action is working, but it is working for a select group, it is working for white women....

Lisa's account coincides with W. E. B. Du Bois's poignant description more a century ago of the veil that shuts out stigmatized groups from society at large as well as from full participation in the workplace. Du Bois identifies the split in consciousness between how one is viewed externally and one's true identity, between one's American identity and one's ascriptive characteristics. In this chapter, we shall see how this dialectical dichotomy or double consciousness of stigmatized groups still persists in the higher education workplace, as substantiated by the research literature and the intensive, qualitative interviews conducted for this study. The veil of discrimination obstructs the participation of stigmatized groups in their day-to-day work environment and creates a double bind. The veil symbolizes antagonism and interdependence, linking the small-scale or micro-events in the work environment with the large-scale or macro-dimensions of social life (Winant, 2004).

Viewed differently within the workplace, minorities, women, and LGBT professionals must contend with their own "two-ness" or even multiplicity of identities and still keep their careers intact. Overarching and underpinning these workplace experiences is the predominance of the centuries-old "white racial frame" (Feagin, 2010b). The white racial frame that still represents this nation's dominant frame of reference is composed of five main components: 1) racial stereotypes (beliefs aspect); 2) racial narratives and interpretations (cognitive aspect); 3) racial images (visual aspect) and language accents (auditory aspect); 4) racialized emotions (feelings aspect); and 5) inclination to discriminatory acts (Feagin, 2010b). Emotions associated with this racial frame include a sense of racial superiority, racial hatred, racial arrogance, and a desire for dominance over others (Feagin, 2010b). In the ethnographic observation of discrimination in the workplace chronicled in this chapter, we will see evidence of emotional tyranny—the use of emotion by powerful organization members through an emotional weaponry of language, tactics, and nonverbal display, often in public settings (Waldron, 2009).

Power imbalance and the hierarchical distribution of authority in the university's administrative environment heighten the potential for discriminatory treatment. While a significant number of research studies have broken new ground in examining stress arising from discrimination as well as coping responses, most studies do not address how structural inequities related to job security, authority, and stability raise the stakes for marginalized groups by amplifying the impact of perceived discrimination. And despite the fact that social psychologists have studied stigmas for over forty years, only recently has stigma theory been recognized as a significant theoretical anchor for studying diversity and discrimination in organizations (Ragins, Singh, and Cornwell, 2007). In this context, we explore the interrelationship of discrimination, stress, and health outcomes within the context of asymmetric power relations in the university workplace.

Furthermore, we introduce the "minority stress model" in this chapter to examine the consequences of perceived discrimination nested within the context of asymmetrical power relationships and hierarchical organizational structures within the university. Through exploration of how forms of psychological domination can occur, we consider the growing body of empirical research on the relation of discrimination to physical and mental health. To counteract forms of perceived discrimination, the discussion centers upon the development of counter frames of resistance, including approaches suggested by administrators interviewed in our study. These practical resistance strategies provide a repertoire of approaches to help women, minorities, and LGBT administrators protect self-esteem, sustain equilibrium on a day-to-day basis, and respond resiliently to subtle forms of marginalization. Indeed, responses to perceived discrimination must be adjusted based upon fluctuating circumstances. Individual prioritizing and activation of goals, self-appraisal, and evaluation of available options are essential considerations for diverse professionals seeking to maintain equilibrium in challenging environments (Swim and Thomas, 2006).

The Intersection of Daily Work Experiences and the Process of Discrimination

Three research studies provide salient examples of the intersection of the dynamic process of discrimination with everyday work experience based upon race and gender. An analysis of 60,743 workplace race and sex discrimination cases filed with the Ohio Civil Rights Commission from 1988 to 2003 revealed disparate policing by gatekeeping actors of minority employees in formalized procedures through differential application of policies (Roscigno, 2007; Roscigno, Garcia, and Bobbitt-Zeher, 2007). The study also found managerial discretion and use of particularistic criteria influenced the evaluation process of who to hire and promote and identified differential treatment of minorities and women on the job in day-to-day workplace interactions expressed through covert and overt forms of harassment (Roscigno, Garcia, and Bobbitt-Zeher, 2007).

A second comprehensive study analyzed interview data from over two hundred middle-class African Americans and exploratory focus groups with economically successful African Americans to document the physical, psychological, and family/community costs of everyday racism in the workplace (Feagin and McKinney, 2003). Interview accounts revealed forms of "woodwork" racism or incidents that might seem small and unimportant to outside white observers, yet cause great pain and stress to minorities (Feagin and McKinney, 2003). Several themes of this study are consistent with the interviews of administrators cited in this chapter: the tendency of white participants and bystanders to make light of hostile harassment; the view of many white Americans that discrimination can be undertaken with little or no form of punishment; the tendency to blame the victims of discrimination; and the ambiguity of informal rules that allows institutionalized racism to persist (Feagin and McKinney, 2003).

Although on a much smaller scale, a third research study used the interpretive methodology of daily diaries to capture the everyday, interactive process of subtle discriminatory action, finding that undergraduate women participants encountered one to two sexist incidents per week, through gender role stereotypes, demeaning comments and behaviors, and sexual objectification (Swim, Hyers, Cohen, and Ferguson, 2001).

The entry of women, minorities, and LGBT administrators into traditionally white, male-dominated leadership roles can generate stress for these individuals and trigger everyday incidents with profound psychological ramifications for the targets. From a macro-level, the sociocultural context surrounding American higher education is the backdrop for day-to-day situations of exclusion and marginalization, since until only recently colleges and universities focused almost exclusively on the education of white, upper- and middle-class male students (Tierney, 2008). The predominance of white male administrators and faculty still perpetuates and reinforces existing social hierarchies within the daily context of educational institutions. From a micro-political level, we shall see in this chapter the way acts of *social closure* transpire through the medium of institutional processes and the agency of gatekeeping actors that both create and reinforce disparities (Roscigno, 2007). Social closure is a concept developed by Max Weber that refers to the effort to maximize rewards by restricting access to opportunities and rewards to a limited eligible group (Elliott and Smith, 2001).

Those in power define reality within the cultural setting of the university. As a key element of social oppression, the dominant group has the power to name reality as well as determine what is "correct," "normal," and "real" (Hardiman and Jackson, 1997). And demographic variables function as "building blocks" in the social construction of individual power within these organizational settings (Bacharach, Bamberger, and Mundell, 2006). From a behavioral perspective, a particular belief or behavior has greater impact when it comes from a person in power, since material implications of behaviors between the powerful and historically disadvantaged are asymmetrical also (Prasad, Pringle, and Konrad, 2006).

Institutional culture and ethos can sustain stereotypical ideas and biased attitudes through a complex interweaving set of systems, principles, and practices beneath a seemingly egalitarian veneer (Rangasamy, 2004). These practices reinforce the subtle stigmatization of certain groups that can transpire even through the subtle medium of institutional language. Specifically, the articulation and naming of certain realities by the dominant group in power enables things to occur in specific ways through ownership of institutional language and the status quo (Rangasamy, 2004).

Since perceived competence is an important ingredient of power, stereotypes relating to minority groups are antithetical to the attainment of power and result in both the maintenance of existing group power relations as well as the use of the characteristics of the dominant group to define power (Ragins, 1997). In this respect, stereotypes of diverse groups can be distorted to reflect characteristics that are antithetical to dominant power perceptions such as being weak, lacking initiative, and being nurturing or incompetent (Ragins, 1997). Perceptions of power are influenced by stereotypes, prototypical views, and attributions that can further influence the acquisition and development of power (Ragins and Sundstrom, 1989).

The relationship between rank and power also differs for members of minority and majority groups, with minorities less likely to hold the power associated with the positions they occupy (see Ragins, 1997, for review). Clear findings indicate that blacks are less likely than whites to exercise authority in the workplace in terms of broad supervisory control over others including pay, promotions, and hiring, while men have significantly greater authority return for educational investments than women (see Smith, 2002, for review). Even when a minority group member attains positional power, this power may be more vulnerable to attack and less stable than majority group members, due to biased attributions (Ragins, 1997). In this regard, a study of 828 managers in three companies revealed that black managers reported lower levels of job discretion and acceptance in their roles than white managers, and were also rated lower in job performance and promotability assessments (Greenhaus, Parasuraman, and Wormley, 1990).

Returning to Lisa's account at the opening of this chapter, differential role expectations coupled with a lack of resources and support thwart the career success of newly hired minority and female professionals. As Lisa further explains:

> What people don't realize when they're working with minorities, and in some cases women, is that you are using a yardstick you would never use if it was someone you brought in, that you know, who is just like you. So you changed the yardstick. The person doesn't know you changed it, and you probably don't even know you are doing it. So everything that they are doing, you are judging it on a higher level than you would even judge yourself. So when you do an evaluation, of course they are going to fail. They are probably even going to fail even before you did the evaluation....
>
> I feel like some people are getting Obama jobs, meaning OK, you totally screwed it up. You have a chance now that you are finally going to use your diversity draw, so bring in the black woman to fix it. In Obama's case, bring him in. What do you expect that person to do that is going to be magical? All of a sudden, you got into the diversity thing. So magically, they are going to fix all the problems that someone else has screwed up. It happens at institutions all along. What it does, it gives the people who do the hiring the opportunity to say, 'OK, we hired one and she failed.' Well why? And also we put those people in those positions and don't give them the resources to actually address the problems. And what I am led to believe is you weren't really interested in fixing it from the start. You hire the person to say you did it, and they fail, and you can say, 'OK, now you understand why we don't hire them.'

Lisa's description of the challenges faced by new minority hires replicates the self-defeating diversity recruitment cycle identified by Roosevelt Thomas (Thomas, 1990). First, institutions recognize the need for diversity and have great expectations for diversity hires (Thomas, 1990). However, once hired, minorities and women experience frustration, leading eventually to dormancy and a silent front by the institution, followed by crisis and the revolving door (Thomas, 1990). And, as a minority female administrator, Lisa speaks of the constant concern that any small mistakes she makes will be magnified and used disproportionately to evaluate her performance:

> I have had some situations where I was trying to control time schedules, control everyone else's time schedule, control my own, you know, trying to perform magic, where I, and maybe I was being an overachiever, but I think the reason I would go out of my way, or the times I have gone out of my way to control everything around me, because I believe that it is viewed differently if I let a ball drop. Everyone pays attention if I let a ball drop. Whereas the mainstream white male or white female drops a ball, no one even looks in that direction.

Similarly, Mark, an Asian American administrator, reports the application of a double standard with severe consequences for diverse professionals. Exaggeration of actions taken by targeted individuals coupled with a lack of supervisory direction or feedback can result in expulsion or dismissal. Mark relates how such actions evolved on his campus: "I think there are several situations that were perceived by colleagues on campus that involves potentially a double standard and lacking in clarity leading to their dismissal or being taken too seriously into account. The situations are different enough that I would think that it is not uncommon for folks to feel that they have not been instructed by their supervisors ... but later on held responsible. This happens often enough."

Power begets power through a synergistic process that involves the compounding of *vertical* levels of power through relationships with supervisors and subordinates and *horizontal* lines of power through peers (Ragins and Sundstrom, 1989). As a result, subordinate groups may not be able to capitalize upon synergies of power, not only because of limitations in vertical relationships (upward influence on supervisors and downward influence on subordinates), but also due to horizontal relationships with peers.

In this regard, Jennifer, a Latina administrator, notes the behavioral barriers and lack of respect that minorities and women experience in vertical relationships through day-to-day interactions with colleagues. She explains how the acceptance of messages varies based upon the race, gender, ethnicity, and even accent of the messenger. Lisa's account of a meeting in which her contributions were ignored despite her expertise in a given area illustrates how micro-incursions of omission and misrecognition occur in everyday settings. While minorities and women are in one sense highly visible, in another sense they can be treated as if they are invisible within decision-making forums. As Jennifer observes:

> There have been times clearly where I have had to work to ensure that other people have kind of applied a respectful tone and behavior in situations. Sometimes very, very, very subtle, but very noticeable to me clearly and very noticeable to others....
>
> I can remember being in a meeting, and I'm Latina, and we were discussing outreach to Latino communities in different departments and I expressed a concern because I thought that some of the information being handed out should be revised ... a little bit, in order to allow for maybe it to be a little more receptive to certain communities and was kind of flatly dismissed. You know, 'Oh but we've done the research and we know.' I said, 'I understand but I'm telling you in the places that I look and the people that we speak to....' And basically kind of not paid attention to. And then you know a different person in the room saying, 'Well we've gone to the conference, and we heard x....' ... I'm talking to a wall, where no one is paying attention or listening. I use what I call message and messenger. And there are some messages that people have very difficult times listening to the messenger.... And it happens I think more often with certain groups than others, based on race and ethnicity, you know, accents, national origin, gender....

Not being able to connect as an equal in the workplace limits access to important psychological, social, and material benefits offered by the dominant group including relationships and group membership (McLaughlin-Volpe, 2006). It also restricts opportunity for self-definition and self-expansion (McLaughlin-Volpe, 2006). Self-determination is a key feature of the concept of reciprocal empowerment which also emphasizes the principles of collaboration, democratic participation, and distributive justice (Prilleltensky and Gonick, 1994). Self-determination ensures that individuals do not need to revise their identities, and can participate in a workplace culture characterized by dignity and respect (Chun and Evans, 2009).

The Minority Stress Model and the Impact of Social Stigma in the Workplace

Diverse administrators face special challenges due to the daily tightrope they walk in academe and the heightened consequences of missteps. Balancing the demands of academic life with the multi-marginality that derives from under-representation creates significant stress in the effort to perform and succeed within the university environment (Thompson and Dey, 1998). The stress created from this balancing act is often not anticipated by individuals and is acknowledged by few observers, especially in light of publicly articulated diversity goals of the university (Thompson and Dey, 1998).

A growing and significant body of research identifies perceived discrimination as a unique source of major and chronic stress separate from everyday life stresses that affect the mental and physical health of its targets (Flores et al., 2008; Meyer, 2003; Waldo, 1999; Wei, Ku, Russell, Mallinckrodt, and Liao, 2008). Researchers have developed the *minority status stress* model to describe the stress caused by discrimination and have theorized that multiple disadvantaged social categories such as race, gender, and sexual orientation expose individuals to risk factors that increase vulnerability to stress and compromise health (Flores et al., 2008; Meyer, 1995; Meyer, 2003; Waldo, 1999; Williams, Lavizzo-Mourey, and Warren, 1994). Minority stress has been defined as psychosocial stress related to stigmatization in a minority status (Meyer, 1995).

The experience of stigma essentially implies a threat to the self, to the desired self-image, and to self-esteem (Crocker and Garcia, 2006). As a discrediting experience, the phenomenon of stigma involves rejection. Such rejection occurs through devaluation of characteristics such as race, gender, and sexual orientation, subjecting targeted individuals to stressors resulting from prejudiced attitudes and discriminatory practices (Crocker and Garcia, 2006; Lewis, Derlega, Clarke, and Kuang, 2006; Mendoza-Denton, Page-Gould, and Pietrzak, 2006; Miller, 2006). Possessing a stigmatized or devalued social identity is similar to other types of acute and chronic stressors (Major, 2006).

From this vantage point, minority status stress derives from the in-congruence between a stigmatized person's needs and experience with social structures and behaviors that tax or even exceed adaptive resources (Meyer, 1995; Miller, 2006). Targets of harassment often experience multiple forms of mistreatment, including harassment based on their social identity group (e.g., race, gender, sexual orientation, disability) and generalized workplace harassment (Raver and Nishii, 2010). Workplace harassment is detrimental to employees' well-being, giving rise to immediate physiological responses such as increased heart rate and blood pressure, which may lead to longer-term strain (see Raver and Nishii, 2010 for review).

The minority stress model identifies three processes of stress: 1) external stressful events; 2) the expectation of such events that requires additional vigilance; and 3) the internalization of negative social attitudes (Meyer, 2003). Furthermore, research by Mendoza-Denton and colleagues indicates that the anticipation of status-based rejection can give rise to *race-based rejection sensitivity* (RS-race) and *prejudice apprehension* that causes individuals to perceive discrimination more quickly and to react more intensely (Mendoza-Denton, Page-Gould, and Pietrzak, 2006).

One researcher, for example, identifies five types of racism-related stress that also can be generalized to the discrimination faced by women and LGBT individuals: 1) major life events; 2) vicarious experiences of racism through friends, family, and others; 3) daily micro-stressors; chronic-contextual forms of stress through institutionalized forms of racism; 4) collective experiences of racism; and 5) transgenerational transmission of trauma experienced by the group (Harrell, 2000). These interactions can diminish an individual's cognitive and emotional resources or threaten well-being in terms of physical, psychological, social, functional, and spiritual resources (Harrell, 2000).

In particular, the process of replaying a situation in one's mind again and again, questioning one's own perceptions and reactions, trying to explain it to others, and examining alternative explanations sometimes creates even more stress beyond the original experience (Pierce, 1995). The effect of some experiences upon ethnic minorities through physical and verbal attacks has been described as a contemporary form of *lynching* that has a documented negative effect on health outcomes (Karlsen and Nazroo, 2002). Another researcher identifies the humiliation dynamic in racism that can occur by targeted "invidious" attention to an individual or through systematically ignoring the victim and making him or her invisible (Griffin, 1991).

Stigmatized individuals face significant risk in identifying attributions of discrimination since these judgments threaten the dominant ideology (Kaiser, 2006). This risk derives from the predominant belief in a just system as articulated in *system justification theory*. System justification theory refers to the psychological process by which people justify existing social arrangements as fair and legitimate, such as the meritocratic belief that hard work, motivation, and effort lead to success (Jost and Banaji, 1994; Jost and Hunyady, 2002). Prescriptive norms of autonomy, personal control, and self-reliance indicate that individuals must take personal responsibility for outcomes and locate the cause of events within personal attributes (Kaiser, 2006). Attributions to discrimination challenge these norms, creating heightened discomfort, uncertainty, and threat that can be relieved by punishing the source of the threat (see Kaiser, 2006, for review).

The impact of social stigma in the higher education workplace is a significant source of stress for diverse administrators. Consistent with the minority stress model, Mark, the Asian American administrator cited earlier, describes how everyday psychological stress arises from the need to continually gauge how his actions will be received. Unpredictability makes stressors even more stressful and heightens vigilance (Sapolsky, 1998). Mark emphasizes the ongoing and cumulative nature of this anticipatory stress:

> Well I think, it is always the psychological stress that comes from ... you feel you have to always been reading what is appropriate for you to do or say ... figuring out what is appropriate and gauging that before you do something. The effect may or may not be due to who we are in terms of race, gender. But it happens to us. Psychologically, inevitably, race comes in, gender comes in, sexual orientation comes in, religion comes in, all right in a Catholic institution, that is part of our own assessment and anxiety about who we are in these environments. It presents an ongoing stressor in our everyday lives and has a cumulative effect.

In addition, Mark explains how the complexity and ambiguity of workplace situations lends itself to different interpretations. Due to the clandestine and often veiled nature of subtle discrimination, complex situations provide opportunity for observers to overlook or downplay exclusionary acts and behaviors. Diverse individuals are often unclear themselves as to the role played by race, gender, or sexual orientation in such actions. In a telling statement, Mark articulates the antagonistic position that race places him in within the university environment. This statement reveals the everyday expression of the stratification of privilege—the collision of systems of power and daily workplace reality. Under these circumstances, Mark explains that considerations of race and difference must always be in the background for diverse administrators:

> Situations tend to be fairly complex, and the frustrating part is when we feel [we are] being wronged it is very hard to reduce the situation to simply right and wrong. And it is usually complex enough that there could be different interpretations. And we may not win all the time. In fact we don't because of the complexity of the situation. As a person of color, clearly I feel that one way or the other [it] put[s] me in a kind of perpetually antagonistic position with other people. Race, for me, always is in the background. Whether it is real or not, it's part of my assessment, and it always weighs heavily in terms of my own psyche. And I think that's true for many of our colleagues of color that you never know for sure whether who you are contributed to a decision.

Given systemic inequalities and the prevailing view of the system as just and meritocratic, taking an activist role in an institution can be especially hazardous for minorities, women, and LGBT individuals. As Mark further relates, a couple of minority deans were terminated, in part because of the activist role they played in trying to establish a cross-cultural studies program. Ironically, such a program would have provided increased support for minority faculty, administrators, and staff:

> It's when I left, an African American dean was fired and another was pushed out. Those of us who were involved in it, we achieved the results that we wanted, but in some ways it's a casualty to folks who were activists—senior administrators who were activists in the process of achieving this goal. Not only did we left [sic] for a variety of reasons, the faculty members who were involved also left. In the end, the majority of the faculty and administrators who were involved in this left within five years. Administration tends to see a group of individuals as moving in a direction that they don't like. Yeah, in a sense it is race-related, because we are all people of color in senior positions, but it is not race-related if you look at it from the context of creating institutional change.... We tend to be maintainers of the status quo. But to play an activist role in any institution tends to be hazardous for whatever reason.

Recall the examples in Chapter 1 of two administrators responsible for diversity and affirmative action who were fired from research universities and how the guise of budgetary savings and reorganization was used to justify closure actions. These examples of the dismissal of the individuals responsible for diversity bear striking similarity to the story shared by Alex, a Hispanic male administrator, who served as Chief Diversity Officer at a large research university. Alex recounts how his role was not taken seriously, how he was frozen out of the communications process and how his position was eliminated. The sudden removal of the highest ranking officers responsible for diversity and inclusion in the university reflect the emboldened view of gatekeeping actors that acts of discrimination can be undertaken with few, if any, consequences. As Alex relates: "A scandal unrelated to my position as chief diversity officer became the central concern of my institution's central administration. I continued to advocate for diversity and soon became an isolated and inconvenient voice. Before long, my position was eliminated. It confirmed what I had figured out soon after I was hired, that the creation of my position was just intended as diversity window dressing and little more."

In another example, Joan, a white human resources administrator, describes the chilly climate for minorities in a small university town as well as the fear and stress generated among African American and female employees when her university recently announced significant layoffs. As concrete evidence of the minority stress model, minorities and women anticipated the potential for disparate treatment in the university's actions and were concerned and afraid. Joan describes the psychological impact of the announcement of layoffs on minority and female employees:

> There's a broad belief, and I share that belief, on campus ... that people of color are not overtly discriminated against, they are just not as welcome. It's a small town, you know, people form their cliques, and I think that that's true. I think it is hard to break into. I can see it sometimes play out in this small community.... In terms of on-campus activity, I don't experience it myself so much, but I have had people come and talk to me about it.... That there's a sense ... that people of color, gender equity and all that, are just not as welcome.
>
> We had layoffs for the first time ... massive layoffs. We had sixty-five people that lost their jobs. And of course everyone was concerned and afraid they were going to lose their jobs. But the people who came to me, who were so afraid that they had to come to HR to talk about it and figure out if they had to make other plans were predominantly African American or

female.... But my experience was that the people who were so stressed that they felt like they had to come to HR were female and African American. They wanted to know how the decisions would be made.

Clearly, as these examples demonstrate, the impact of social stigma as it intersects with employment creates a double and higher standard for diverse individuals that can result in dire, life-changing consequences, threatening job security and career progress. Negative employment actions are undertaken precipitously, with little regard for the psychological and physical costs to the individual, impact on career progress, and the radiating effects upon family and community. In the next section, we shall continue examination of these themes, as we explore how forms of psychological abuse take place in situations of power imbalance and ambiguous working conditions without organizational safeguards.

Bullying and Forms of Psychological Abuse

Workplace design, hierarchical power structures as well as ambiguous, unorganized situations with no realistic or viable opportunity for redress give rise to the potential for bullying of diverse professionals in the higher education workplace. Bullying behaviors flourish in situations of power and powerlessness, particularly when vulnerable targets have limited access to defenses within a situational context (see Einarsen and Skogstad, 1996; Keashly, 1998; LaVan and Martin, 2008; Roscigno, Lopez, and Hodson, 2009). Bullying may be motivated by racism, sexism, or heterosexism, but beyond that, bullies find diverse individuals easy targets whom they can ostracize or isolate, since these individuals already are faced with isolation in the workplace (Roscigno, Lopez, and Hodson, 2009).

Key characteristics of bullying include *repeated* and *cumulative* behaviors in a constellation of both verbal and nonverbal acts with hostile intent, which can be presented in a subtle and less detectable manner (Einarsen, 1999; Einarsen, Hoel, Zapf, and Cooper, 2003; Keashly, 1998; Lutgen-Sandvik, Namie, and Namie, 2009; McAvoy and Murtagh, 2003; Wornham, 2003). Systematic mistreatment takes shape in an escalating continuum of psychological pressure followed by psychological harassment and emotional abuse reinforced by repetition (Einarsen, Hoel, Zapf, and Cooper, 2003; Rayner, Hoel, and Cooper, 2002). Bullying actions may involve constant criticism, reduction of professional status, threats, isolation, overwork, and destabilization (Rayner and Hoel, 1997; Wornham, 2003).

The *victim-perpetrator-guardian model* developed by researchers after review of 204 book-length organizational ethnographies finds that women, minorities, and those with little job security are at greater risk for being targets of bullying, especially in situations of organizational chaos, ambiguity, or confusion (Roscigno, Lopez, and Hodson, 2009). A study of eighty-two book-length workplace ethnographies in the United States and England found three types of workplaces: contentious workplaces characterized by systematic, ongoing interpersonal conflict; cohesive workplaces with limited conflict or abuse; and unorganized workplaces with chaotic organization (Roscigno and Hodson, 2004). A disorganized workplace creates stress and uncertainty, magnifying the potential for bullying and harassment.

Similar to the concept of indentured servitude described earlier, parallels can be drawn with forms of psychological domination such as those Hall describes with regard to black conservatism as an extension of plantation hierarchy (Hall, 2008). A central aspect of such domination is proximity to the master as well as dependency on the master—or *rooming in the master's house* (Hall, 2008). The proximity and dependency characteristic of employment situations for diverse university professionals heightens the potential for subtle forms of psychological abuse, due to the absence of recourse and regulation.

We return now to Claudia's account cited at the opening of the book. When Claudia's supervisor, a white male, called her an "Oreo" in an open university meeting, Claudia, an African American female administrator, told him that most people would consider that a racial slur. His reply was, "Oh, I don't mean that. You are one of them that has common sense." Subsequently, Claudia went to speak with him about the incident, realizing clearly how he felt about her due to her race. She explains:

> But he was beginning now to say things openly about me. Oh well. You know, he would ask these stupid questions like 'How do black people feel about … (whatever topic we were discussing).' And I said to him, 'I don't know. I can only tell you how this one black woman feels. Because everyone is an individual.' And I pointed out to him that no one goes to him and says 'How do white people feel about things?' I can't speak for the whole race.

Although she had been employed at the institution for several years, Claudia's supervisor began to refuse to accept her appointments and would not take her calls, providing her no direction or feedback. Yet, in a clear abuse of authority, he would call her at 11:00 p.m. to harass her by giving her assignments due the following morning at 8:00 a.m. These behaviors caused her to be continually vigilant and under constant stress. Claudia recounts how the escalation of her supervisor's actions led to constant stress:

> I was always stressed out, always worried about watching my back, trying to figure out what he was going to find wrong with every little thing that I did. So, I mean, I stayed up many nights working. In fact, he used to call me at 11:00 at night saying I need this report on my desk tomorrow at 8:00 in the morning and that would be the only time he would ever ask for it was at 11:00 at night. But he did things to really just get to me and try to push me to the edge. And he almost succeeded. I guess once he decided that he truly could not work with me he avoided me; I could not get an appointment with him. When he first became my supervisor, he took my calls. I was able to see him on a regular basis. We had regular meetings.... And I guess I must have used one too many teachable moments. And he was done.

The supervisor's passive-aggressive behavior was designed to just fly under the institutional radar, yet as she describes it, "push her to the edge." Claudia further relates how this situation coupled with an effort to involve her in what she perceived to be in an unethical directive eventually led to the termination of her employment without warning in an undignified fashion, with security escorting her off campus:

> There were a number of things that happened. Some had to do with discrimination and some had to do with a difference in integrity issues. There were some things that I was asked to do that I felt were unethical. And so I had a discussion with him and asked him about the directive and explained to him why I thought there might be a problem. And I asked him for clarification. He was very angry that I questioned him and basically kicked me out of his office. Then he called me in about a week later, offered me a significant salary increase if I would join him in this venture. I declined and soon thereafter, about a week thereafter he called me to his office and told me that he was accepting my resignation. I never did resign. But I told him, you know, he would have no problem out of me. I left and didn't look back.
>
> I figured at that point it didn't really matter to me because he was going to put in the file whatever he was going to put in there. I had no say

so over it. He told me that it was my last day and in fact I was escorted off campus [by security]. I took my things and I left. I went on with my life and moved forward and my life has been much better since I left.

The ambiguity of the administrative work environment coupled with the virtually unchallenged nature of power without countervailing forces allowed Claudia's supervisor to pursue a course of progressive and systematic bullying without scrutiny or intervention. This example illustrates how the absence of a guardian in the victim-perpetrator-guardian model allowed a progressive course of harassment resulting in termination. Due to the difficulty of proving discrimination under existing civil rights statutes, the high costs of litigation, economic necessity, and the importance of preserving one's career path and ability to be rehired, administrators subjected to psychological abuse frequently elect not to pursue legal redress. As such cases unfold, given the lack of ability to protest and the absence of workplace protections, the likelihood of the continuation of such acts of discrimination increases. As a result, the individuals perpetrating these actions may come to believe that they can undertake systematic mistreatment of diverse individuals with impunity.

The Impact of Discrimination on Mental and Physical Health

Significant research links experiences of discriminatory mistreatment to adverse health impacts persisting over a significant period of time. Stigmatized individuals, like everyone else, have limited resources available to them, yet face the same stressors others face plus those created by prejudice (Miller, 2006). Trying to cope with everything may leave stigmatized individuals unable to cope with anything (Miller, 2006). In this regard, recent research indicates that at the heart of ethnic health vulnerabilities is differential exposure to psychosocial stressors due to insufficient access to or control over material, social, and psychological resources (Myers, Lewis, and Parker-Dominguez, 2003).

Two categories of stressors create differential vulnerability: subjective factors such as perceived discrimination and blocked opportunity as well as objective statuses through negative major events including unemployment, loss of status, and other hardships (Vega and Rumbaut, 1991). The unavailability of means for reaching valued goals can have destructive consequences for minorities who persist in efforts to counteract racist systems and may be psychologically vulnerable if they are unsuccessful (see Vega and Rumbaut, 1991, for review). Compounding these issues, when minority group members accept the "stigma of inferiority," this psychological attack on the ego identity can lead to impaired psychological functioning (Williams and Williams-Morris, 2000, p. 243).

Most strikingly, over the past 150 years, African Americans have higher rates of death, disease, and disability than whites have, and have higher levels of psychological distress and lower levels of subjective well-being (see Williams, Yu, Jackson, and Anderson, 1997, for review). In this regard, findings from the longitudinal study of cardiovascular risk factors (CARDIA) among 1,722 African American adults over a period of fifteen years clearly associate perceived discrimination at work with worse mental and physical health in both men and women (Borrell, Kiefe, Williams, Diez-Roux, and Gordon-Larsen, 2006). The study also found a stronger association of worse mental and physical health in women that could be explained through the double jeopardy that occurs through the compounding of sex discrimination (Borrell, Kiefe, Williams, Diez-Roux, and Gordon-Larsen, 2006).

A longitudinal study of 1,778 working women substantiated the emotional and physical costs of discrimination including 30 percent higher distress rates and chronic physical health problems that appear several years after discrimination is reported (Pavalko, Mossakowski, and Hamilton, 2003). In addition, a study of 2,095 Asian American adults conducted between 2002 and 2003 found self-reported discrimination to be a consistent and "robust" predictor of having any anxiety or depressive disorder (Gee, Spencer, Chen, Yip, and Takeuchi, 2007, p. 1992). This study emphasizes the "common causal pathway" between discrimination and mental disorders (Gee, Spencer, Chen, Yip, and Takeuchi, 2007, p. 1992). A structural model developed by researchers in a study of 520 African American adults found racist discrimination composed of recent racist events, lifetime racist events, and appraised discrimination was a strong predictor of blacks' psychiatric symptoms, above and beyond contextual factors of education, age, and income (Klonoff, Landrine, and Ullman, 1999).

A dozen community studies conducted between 1987 and 2000 that involved minorities as well as gay men found a positive association between discrimination and psychological distress (Williams and Williams-Morris, 2000). Meyer's (1995) community study of 741 New York City gay men found discrimination and stigmatization predictive of psychological distress and associated with a two- to threefold increase in risk for high distress levels (Meyer, 1995). A study of fifty-three male-to-female transgendered individuals showed that fears related to being transsexual and of losing significant relationships such as employment was a strong predictor of psychological distress (Sanchez and Vilain, 2009).

Returning to Claudia's narrative cited earlier, she describes the physical effects of the stress she encountered from the psychological abuse of her supervisor. The impact of her mistreatment and the cumulative impact of stress had profound physical effects that threatened her ability to survive. As Claudia relates:

> When I had that very discriminatory supervisor, I had extremely high blood pressure. I was on three medications. They were at the maximum dosage and my blood pressure was still uncontrollable. My doctor kept telling me I needed to quit my job because he said I was going to die. He said I was going to just have a stroke or heart attack because my blood pressure was so high. After I was terminated, I started to almost faint, and what we found out was that I was on too much medication. And today I don't even take any medication. It was clearly the stress from that job. I am in a similar position but I work for someone who is extremely supportive, who stands beside me, who recognizes that when I make a recommendation it is usually valid, and he's quite supportive. So the difference is huge and I don't have any problems with the blood pressure. Psychologically I can go home now in the evenings and … I find that when I'm leaving work I realize, Oh, I have had an enjoyable day. I didn't use to experience that.

Similarly, Jennifer, the Latina administrator cited earlier, describes how increasing stress led to illness and eventually the departure of another Latina administrator from the university due to isolation, lack of support, and negative feedback. As Jennifer explains:

> And another administrator I can think of who was not successful and left our institution this year. She definitely went out on a medical leave as a result of the stress and kind of the negative comments and you know, she is a Latina female. The person she was having problems with was a white male. Her boss was a white male for some time and [her boss] then changed to a white female. And you know the dynamic in that whole situation led her to leave on a medical leave. Negative comments, basically … kind of

given a lot of work to do but with not a lot of support. Lack of communication ... not being invited and included in certain things ... and ... feeling very isolated as a result of that. She described things as being very cliquish around her. And was stressed, completely stressed, mentally, physically.... She went on medical leave and then actually the program she was a part of was eliminated. And so ... they were working to provide her with an alternative job assignment but she chose to leave the university.

The impact of inequitable work situations on psychological health is further documented by Megin, a white female administrator, who describes her exclusion from a major decision-making role at the university table despite her hard work and significant contributions, while white males were promoted above her. This situation which she describes as "horrific," led to stress and depression, resulting in her departure from her prior institution:

> ... I feel like I was treated unfairly and to the point where I was in a depression; I was in a depression. And that's not me at all; I am not a person who has experienced that previously. I felt like I worked really, really hard, did a fantastic job, and was still not brought to the head table because I was a woman. And then there were people younger than me, people that were male, people that were white male, that were being promoted above me. And it really was horrific, and that's why I left, that's why I am here now.

These examples clearly illustrate how discriminatory circumstances elude notice within the university community, while affected individuals bear the burden of these actions of inequality, frequently in isolation and without an institutional safety net.

The accounts of diverse administrators who have been the targets of discriminatory practices reveal the serious psychological impact of mistreatment and acts of employment closure. In some cases, the notion of emotional trauma may apply. As targeted groups within society, women, racial minorities, and LGBT individuals are at higher risk of traumatic assault (Tal, 1996). Severe reactions to victimization even can be understood in terms of Post-Traumatic Stress Disorder (PTSD) that involves three components: persistent *re-experiences* of the distress through intrusive thoughts and memories; a *numbing* of responsiveness and avoidance of stimuli associated with trauma; and symptoms of *increased arousal* such as through sleep disturbances and difficulty concentrating (Garnets, Herek, and Levy, 1990). For example, traumatic assault upon individuals with lesbian/gay/bisexual/transgendered sexual orientation through hate-crimes is well documented (Garnets, Herek, and Levy, 1990; Herek, Gillis, and Cogan, 1999). Survivors of such hate-crime victimization exhibited higher levels of depression, post-traumatic stress, and depression (see Szymanski, 2009 for review).

Researchers argue that racist incidents are similar to rape and domestic violence as forms of victimization that produce trauma and are motivated by the imposition of power over those who are less powerful (Bryant-Davis and Ocampo, 2005). In this regard, perpetrators of domestic violence and racist incidents use two main methods of power: economic dependence and isolation of the victim from means of support (Bryant-Davis and Ocampo, 2005).

Due to the limitations of pathologically based PTSD criteria that emphasize physical and life-threatening events, Carter (2007) proposes a non-pathological *race-based traumatic stress* category that acknowledges emotional pain deriving from racial discrimination and harassment (Carter, 2007). Events must be perceived as negative, sudden, and uncontrollable (Carter, 2007). Unlike the dominant American cultural lens that focuses on dispositional characteristics and locates problems in personal failure, race-based traumatic stress recognizes the impact of situational factors that produce trauma (Carter, 2007). The most severe forms of race-based traumatic stress may not result from physical attack, but occur when the psychological pain of experiences produces damage or the threat of damage to the individual's sense of self through memorable, chronic, or cumulative exposure to racism (Carter, 2007).

The severe effects of discrimination in the workplace are often underestimated, unrecognized, and even discounted. In fact, patterns of covert and overt discrimination create differential vulnerability for women, minority, and LGBT administrators through the traumatic impact of sudden, uncontrollable events or the cumulative impact of multiple incidents and micro-aggressions over a long period of time.

The Effects of Discrimination on Self-Esteem

The process of discrimination can threaten to deplete internal psychological resources and pose a threat to self-esteem. Self-esteem is a central feature of the quality of life and subjective experience, powerfully connected to variables influencing day-to-day experiences (Crocker and Blanton, 1999). Global self-esteem refers to feelings of self-worth, self-acceptance, and self-regulation (Crocker and Garcia, 2010).

We opened the chapter with the notion of double consciousness advanced by W. E. B. Du Bois and the sense stigmatized individuals have "of always looking at oneself through the eyes of others, of measuring one's soul by the tape of a world that looks on in amused contempt and pity" (Du Bois, 2003, p. 9). In this regard, psychiatrist Alvin Poussaint (1966) wrote of the dangers of self-hatred in relation to self-esteem:

> Black men and women learn quickly to hate themselves and each other. . . . And, paradoxically, some black men tend to distrust and hate each other more than their white oppressor. There is abundant evidence that racism has left almost irreparable scars on the psyche of Afro-Americans that burden them with an unrelenting, painful anxiety that drives the psyche to reach out for a sense of identity and self-esteem. (Poussaint, 1966, p. 420)

Nearly forty years later, Poussaint noted the formidable mental stresses faced by African Americans in part due to post-traumatic slavery syndrome as well as the twin burdens of poverty and racism (Poussaint and Alexander, 2000).

One of the perils of double consciousness is that such awareness can activate a "hot" emotional system based upon the need to be a person of worth and value with desirable private and public self-image (Crocker, Moeller, and Burson, 2010; Metcalfe and Mischel, 1999). The effort to pursue contingencies of self-worth or domains in which people feel they must succeed to have value and worth as a human being can detract from long-term goals and limit cognitive capacities and self-regulation (Crocker, Moeller, and Burson, 2010). By contrast, a "warm" system is other-directed rather than self-directed in which people hold compassionate goals and a connection to something larger than the self (Crocker, Moeller, and Burson, 2010). Research indicates that the more students base self-esteem on approval by others, the greater the drop in self-esteem after rejection by a same-sex peer (Crocker, Moeller, and Burson, 2010; Park and Crocker, 2008).

Paradoxically, however, research on self-esteem reveals significant differences among minority groups in levels of self-esteem. Theories on the internalization of stigma that evolved over the past fifty years suggested that levels of self-esteem correlate with the level of social devaluation, expecting that groups that are more significantly devalued socially will have lower self-esteem. Yet a meta-analysis using 712 data samples found nearly the opposite pattern: blacks scored the highest in global self-esteem despite being the most negatively stereotyped and devalued, and Asians scored lowest despite being the least negatively stereotyped and devalued (Twenge and Crocker, 2002). From highest to lowest self-esteem scores, the groups are ordered as follows: blacks, whites, Hispanics, American Indians, and Asians (Twenge and Crocker, 2002). These significant findings point to the importance of cultural differences, as well as the clear impact of the civil rights movement with black self-esteem rising dramatically from near zero in the 1950s–1960s to one third of a standard deviation higher than Whites by the 1990s (Twenge and Crocker, 2002).

What mechanisms can protect and buffer the self-esteem of stigmatized individuals from self-stigmatization, internalized oppression, and overreaction to external feedback through a "hot system"? Landmark research in social psychology identified several mechanisms that can buffer the self-esteem of members of oppressed groups from prejudice. One mechanism that can protect self-esteem is attributing negative feedback or poor outcomes to the prejudiced attitudes others may hold to their group (Crocker and Major, 1989). Conversely, a study of 257 female college undergraduates revealed that increased psychological distress resulted when women translated sexist incidents into negative public views about women and then into negative personal views of women and themselves individually (Fischer and Holz, 2007). A second buffering mechanism is the ability to make in-group social comparisons (Crocker and Major, 1989). A third mechanism involves selectively devaluing the domains or regarding these domains as less important for self-definition on which they or their in-group has received negative feedback (Crocker and Major, 1989).

New perspectives seek to reset the dial from views of the stigmatized as caught between a rock and a hard place—the rock representing the need to protect self-esteem at the expense of learning, relationships, and motivation, and the hard place representing the effort to sustain learning, relationships, and motivation at the expense of self-esteem (Crocker and Garcia, 2010). For stigmatized individuals, shifting from concerns about stereotypes others hold and defending the self from devaluation to how they can create desired relationships and contribute to transcendent goals represent important strategies (Crocker and Garcia, 2010). Most importantly, in changing the focus from victim to victor, stigmatized individuals can focus upon concrete ways to create situations in which they are valued and feel valued and in this way become the source of what they wish to experience (Crocker and Garcia, 2010).

A focus on the organization as *ecosystem* rather than *egosystem* in which contributors work synergistically to support others as they pursue valuable institutional goals (Crocker and Garcia, 2010) offers a vision of an administrative workplace characterized by safety, mutual respect, and inclusion.

Resistance Counter Frames: Building a Collective Consciousness

Building a collective consciousness is an important buffer for discriminatory events. To mitigate the effects of discrimination, the ability to bear witness to what has occurred is a form of remembering that helps individuals retain control over the interpretation of the trauma experience and cope with the effects of such discrimination (Tal, 1996). As the literature on self-esteem points out, collective efforts have had great impact on the maintenance of self-esteem by minority groups. In this regard, the impact of the civil rights movement and the development of a refined collective consciousness has been linked to the rise of self-esteem among black Americans (Twenge and Crocker, 2002). Over centuries of racial oppression, African Americans have developed important counter frames of resistance (Feagin, 2010a). The impact of historically black colleges and universities (HBCUs), African American studies programs, and pan-African movements may also be factors in the establishment of a strong collective consciousness (Twenge and Crocker, 2002).

Other minority groups such as Asian Americans have been less successful in such forms of collective action and consciousness-building. As Frank Wu, author and Chancellor of the University of California Hastings School of Law indicates, Asian Americans occupy a unique position, due to the fact that there are no Asian American public intellectuals (Evans and Chun, 2010).

As a second important approach to building a collective consciousness, "deframing" education provides the opportunity to critically analyze and deconstruct key elements of existing frameworks such as the white racial frame (Feagin, 2010a). By contrast, *reframing* replaces old frameworks with new ones such as the liberty-and-justice framework reflected in the Declaration of Independence or the anti-oppression frame developed by African Americans (Feagin, 2010a). In this regard, the Intergroup Dialogue program developed at the University of Michigan, offers a social justice frame as its core emphasis. Through dialogic encounters, participants reframe experiences through exploration of the web of institutional discrimination and the interaction of social systems of oppression (racism, classism, sexism, and heterosexism) (Zuniga, Nagda, Chesler, and Cytron-Walker, 2007).

A third approach to building a collective consciousness involves sharing traumatic and stressful experiences of stigmatization with caring others. For example, a study of 105 lesbian women found that individuals highest in stigma consciousness who experienced the greatest social constraint in talking about lesbian-related matters reported the highest level of internalized homophobia, bodily symptoms, and thought intrusion (Lewis, Derlega, Clarke, and Kuang, 2006). Discussion of stressful events can help desensitize negative emotions and cognitions related to the stressor and relieve the individual of hiding significant feelings and thoughts (Lewis, Derlega, Clarke, and Kuang, 2006).

Coping strategies take place at three levels: intrapersonal, interpersonal, and institutional (Mendoza-Denton, Page-Gould, and Pietrzak, 2006). Problem-focused strategies address actions that can be taken to minimize the effects of the situation such as through cognitive restructuring to redefine devaluing events or even through challenging discriminatory practices. Emotion-focused strategies involve intrapersonal regulation of emotions to successfully manage the impact of stress (see Evans and Chun, 2007, for review).

Interview responses indicated a predominant emphasis on intrapersonal or interpersonal approaches. By contrast, relatively few organizational strategies were noted by administrators, despite institutional responsibility for areas such as human resources and diversity, suggesting that much work still needs to be done to develop systemic institutional approaches to overcoming subtle discrimination.

Jennifer, a Latina administrator cited earlier, describes her internalized efforts to ensure self-regulation and adaptation as well as her external focus on creating desired circumstances through institutional change. In this regard, Jennifer emphasizes the importance of reaching out for assistance and notes the reluctance some may feel in discussing or identifying the stresses and challenges they face on an everyday basis. As she explains, "And I think part of it is being gentle on myself, getting help when necessary, asking for help, and I think that sometimes we are reluctant to do so, because we are worried that things are never going to change. And so I am kind of trying to be a proponent of, well, if you don't know what the issues are, you can't change them."

Taking a stand with respect to discriminatory incidents that occur is also important, but can have attendant risks. Nonetheless, those affected by subtle discrimination can find ways to deflect such behavior, by drawing attention to it in subtle ways, use of humor, and addressing it as it arises in non-confrontational ways. In this regard, Claudia describes her efforts to stop discriminatory incidents on her campus: "I think it is my responsibility to bring it to the attention when I see it and say 'Hey.' It's almost like sexual harassment, 'Hey that's sexual harassment you shouldn't be doing that.' I can say 'Hey, that's discrimination you shouldn't be saying things like that or you shouldn't be doing things like that.'"

Due to the differential behavioral standard for stigmatized individuals, high-stakes conversations require careful preparation, avoidance of emotionalism, use of facts and statistics conveyed in a non-controversial manner, and monitoring tone of voice since women and minorities can be accused of yelling or raising their voice (Chun, 2010). In day-to-day racial incidents, whites perform a range of roles including protagonists, bystanders, assistants, and dissenters (Picca and Feagin, 2010). And in a study that reviewed thousands of accounts of college students, no more than one percent of these accounts reveals that a least one white person took a strong and dissenting action (Picca and Feagin, 2010). Efforts to break the flow of discriminatory remarks can include registering dissent without direct confrontation, such as through the use of humor, puzzlement, or even feigned ignorance.

For the most part, majority administrators interviewed for the study reported fewer personal discriminatory incidents in comparison with minority administrators. Nonetheless, proactive administrators like Joan, a white human resources administrator, identified the need to find new strategies to deal with subtle forms of discrimination. As she observes:

> Certainly when we see anything overt or anything discriminatory, we act very quickly. But with this kind of thing, it's more of a cultural situation, and to be real frank … , I don't know how to act, I don't know what I can do about it. I find it the most difficult thing to approach. The other aspects that are more appalling or I find them revolting, I know how to address those and I can bring justice to them. For these other micro-things you speak of, I don't know how to bring justice there.

In terms of interpersonal strategies, creating alliances across identity groups provides greater strength and unity for minorities, women, and LGBT administrators. Due to the relative isolation of diverse administrators within the higher ranks of the research university, such alliances enable social comparisons within a broader "in-group." The protective mechanisms described earlier of attributing negative outcomes to discrimination can be activated when participants from different identity groups discuss common experiences of differential treatment. Discussion of coping strategies among members of other out-groups can strengthen individual approaches and provide greater likelihood of success.

The heightened awareness that arises from personal mistreatment can result in efforts to correct institutional practices. Claudia explains how she translates her own experiences of mistreatment into organizational approaches designed to promote successful outcomes in her institution:

> Every time something negative happens to me I think to myself, this is a teachable moment, I can learn something from this, and at the very least it is going to make me stronger. I mean there is an old saying that says 'That which does not kill you makes you stronger.' And I realize when I come out of this, no matter how tough it is when I'm going through it, when I come out on the other side, I am going to be stronger, I am going to be more knowledgeable, I am going to have more compassion and empathy for others who are going to go through this down the line. And I know I am not going to treat people the way I am being treated.... I think that is one reason I went into the field of human resources because I love being part of the success of other people.

As part of the intrapersonal repertoire of responses, both majority and minority administrators indicated a reliance upon mentors and colleagues to help identify internal landmines and solidify positional strength. Strategies noted by participants included studying the dynamics of situations and overcoming challenges to personal authority through demonstrated expertise in their positions.

Concluding Perspectives

This chapter has focused upon the process and dynamics of subtle discrimination as it unfolds in research universities through a review of pertinent research literature and the accounts of diverse administrators. Although covert forms of marginalization and exclusion may appear undetectable to many observers and elude institutional notice, the severe consequences of such forms of discrimination impact long-term career and health outcomes for diverse administrators. The tendency to blame those stigmatized without understanding the circumstances that gave rise to their marginalization and exclusion is common, mirroring the types of blaming actions that occur in relation to women in sexual harassment cases. Too often, the immediate response is to jump to the performance of the stigmatized individual, without understanding the forces of stratification and the opportunities for particularistic treatment that subtle discrimination affords.

Perhaps the delineation between blatant and subtle discrimination must be revisited. In an era of so-called colorblindness, the prevalence of covert forms of discrimination suggests a new taxonomy must be developed to keep pace with how the process of mistreatment has evolved. Given the severe effects of covert discrimination that have been discussed in this chapter, the vocabulary of discrimination may need to merge the concepts of blatant/subtle/covert discrimination into a conceptual framework that recognizes the serious and long-lasting effects of micro-incursions, bullying, and psychological abuse upon stigmatized individuals. Institutional policies and practices must be designed to bring justice, in the words of one administrator, to these hidden realities.

The minority stress model provides an interpretative framework for understanding the physical and mental impact of discriminatory experiences in light of finite personal resources. The narratives of minority administrators reveal how the day-to-day process of subtle discrimination takes place through lack of acceptance in established roles, application of differential standards, loss of vertical and horizontal synergies of power, and ultimately the sudden imposition of negative employment outcomes such as termination and position elimination. Bullying, workplace harassment, embarrassment, and intimidation are part of the emotional weaponry that heighten stress, requiring stigmatized individuals to devote precious mental resources and energy to situational appraisal, flexible coping responses, and anticipation of discriminatory behavior and actions.

Qualitative interview findings reveal that employers frequently use meritocratic justification such as neglect of duty or insubordination to justify negative employment outcomes (Roscigno, 2007). Especially when individuals hold significant administrative responsibility, budgetary concerns are given as the reason for dismissal (Roscigno, 2007). Administrative actions can take place suddenly and with little warning or preliminary feedback. Due to the lack of employment protections, the need to preserve a viable career path and reputation, as well as sheer economic necessity, diverse administrators are frequently reluctant to pursue legal remedies.

To a much lesser extent, white female participants reported occasional marginalizing experiences, generally not of the same magnitude as their minority counterparts. Serious concerns about the confidentiality of the interviews were raised by participants, highlighting further the precariousness of their administrative employment status and risks of participation. Nonetheless, the candor of the interviewees reflected a genuine desire to improve working conditions, and as one minority administrator put it, to provide the guidelines for administrators that he had never received.

We have also examined the formation of resistance frameworks and avenues to building a collective consciousness. The development of compassionate goals in support of a holistic ecosystem rather than defending the self from devaluation represents an important approach to protecting global self-esteem. And the emergence of a very significant social psychological literature on coping responses to discrimination should provide valuable insights to individuals facing exclusionary situations.

Nonetheless, despite the valiant efforts and flexible coping approaches employed by stigmatized individuals, much work remains to be done in bringing twenty-first century forms of discrimination to light. Specifically, the dynamics of discrimination in higher education environments are not commonly understood or recognized, particularly in terms of the employment conditions of the growing class of university administrators. Without employment protections, unionization, or other countervailing forces such as activist boards of trustees, formalized alternatives must be found to change the leadership paradigm in the university to ensure greater stability, consistency, and organizational justice. Systemic, university-wide strategies will be needed to increase accountability in institutional processes that permit subjectivity and particularistic treatment. Such transformative institutional approaches will help ensure that the vast resources of talent that women, minorities, and LGBT administrators bring to leadership roles in the research university are not wasted, but contribute to the vitality and success of the university.

In light of the need for systemic strategies for organizational change, in the next chapter we examine the typical structure of university administration in terms of organizational design, reporting relationships, and dominant role-based characteristics in major university sectors. This intensive look at university administrative design will yield deeper insight into change strategies, power dynamics, and the elimination of factors that permit differential treatment in formal organizational processes.

Works Cited

Bacharach, S. B., Bamberger, P., and Mundell, B. (2006). Status inconsistency in organizations: From social hierarchy to stress. *Journal of Organizational Behavior,* 14(1), 21–36.

Borrell, L. N., Kiefe, C. I., Williams, D. R., Diez-Roux, A. V., and Gordon-Larsen, P.

(2006). Self-reported health, perceived racial discrimination, and skin color in African Americans in the CARDIA study. *Social Science & Medicine, 63*(3), 1415–1427.

Bryant-Davis, T., and Ocampo, C. (2005). Racist incident-based trauma. *The Counseling Psychologist, 33*(4), 479–500.

Carter, R. T. (2007). Racism and psychological and emotional injury: Recognizing and assessing race-based traumatic stress. *The Counseling Psychologist, 35*(1), 13–105.

Chun, E. (2010, Winter). Light at the end of the tunnel: Effective responses to difficult dialogues. *Insight into Diversity,* 4.

Chun, E., and Evans, A. (2009). *Bridging the diversity divide: Globalization and reciprocal empowerment in higher education* (ASHE-ERIC Higher Education Reports, Vol. 35, No. 1). San Francisco: Jossey-Bass.

Crocker, J., and Blanton, H. (1999). Social inequality and self-esteem: The moderating effects of social comparison, legitimacy, and contingencies of self-esteem. In T. R. Tyler, R. M. Kramer, and O. P. John (Eds.), *The psychology of the social self* (pp. 171–192). Mahwah, NJ: Lawrence Erlbaum Associates.

Crocker, J., and Garcia, J. A. (2006). Stigma and the social basis of the self: A synthesis. In S. Levin and C. van Laar (Eds.), *Stigma and group inequality: Social psychological perspectives* (pp. 287–208). Mahwah, NJ: Lawrence Erlbaum Associates.

Crocker, J., and Garcia, J. A. (2010). Internalized devaluation and situational threat. In J. J. Dovidio, M. Hewstone, P. Glick, and V. M. Esses (Eds.), *The SAGE handbook of prejudice, stereotyping and discrimination* (pp. 395–409). Thousand Oaks, CA: Sage Publications.

Crocker, J., Moeller, S., and Burson, A. (2010). The costly pursuit of self-esteem: Implications for self-regulation. In R. H. Hoyle (Ed.), *Handbook of personality and self-regulation* (403–429). Malden, MA: Blackwell Publishing.

Crocker, M., and Major, B. (1989). Social stigma and self-esteem: The self-protective properties of stigma. *Psychological Review, 96*(4), 608–630.

Du Bois, W. E. B. (2003). *The souls of black folk.* New York: Barnes & Noble.

Einarsen, S. (1999). The nature and causes of bullying at work. *International Journal of Manpower, 20*(1/2), 16–27.

Einarsen, S., Hoel, H., Zapf, D., and Cooper, C. L. (2003). The concept of bullying at work: The European tradition. In S. Einarsen, H. Hoel, and C. Cooper (Eds.), *Bullying and emotional abuse in the workplace: International perspectives in research and practice* (pp. 3–30). New York: Taylor & Francis.

Einarsen, S., and Skogstad, A. (1996). Bullying at work: Epidemiological findings in public and private organizations. *European Journal of Work and Organizational Psychology, 5*(2), 185–201.

Elliott, J. R., and Smith, R. A. (2001). Ethnic matching of supervisors to subordinate work groups: Findings on "bottom-up" ascription and social closure. *Social Problems, 48*(2), 258–276.

Evans, A., and Chun, E. B. (2007). Copping with behavioral and organizational barriers to diversity in the workplace. *CUPA-HR Journal, 58*(1), 12–18.

Evans, A., and Chun, E. (2010, March). Making it real: Academic leaders of diversity progress. *Insight into Diversity,* 26.

Feagin, J. R. (2010a). *Racist America: Roots, current realities, and future reparations* (2nd ed.). New York: Routledge.

Feagin, J. R. (2010b). *The white racial frame: Centuries of racial framing and counter-framing.* New York: Routledge.

Feagin, J. R., and McKinney, K. D. (2003). *The many costs of racism.* Lanham, MD: Rowman & Littlefield.

Fischer, A. R., and Holz, K. B. (2007). Perceived discrimination and women's psychological distress. *Journal of Counseling Psychology,* 54(2), 154–164.

Flores, E., Tschann, J. M., Dimas, J. M., Bachen, E. A., Pasch, L. A., and de Groat, C. L. (2008). Perceived discrimination, perceived stress, and mental and physical health among Mexican-origin adults. *Hispanic Journal of Behavioral Sciences,* 30(4), 401–424.

Garnets, L., Herek, G. M., and Levy, B. (1990). Violence and victimization of lesbians and gay men: Mental health consequences. *Journal of Interpersonal Violence,* 5(3), 366–383.

Gee, G. C., Spencer, M., Chen, J., Yip, T., and Takeuchi, D. T. (2007). The association between self-reported racial discrimination and 12-month DSM-IV mental disorders among Asian Americans nationwide. *Social Science & Medicine,* 64(10), 1984–1996.

Greenhaus, J. H., Parasuraman, S., and Wormley, W. M. (1990). Effects of race on organizational experiences, job performance evaluations, and career outcomes. *The Academy of Management Journal,* 33(1), 64–86.

Griffin, J. T. (1991). Racism and humiliation in the African American community. *The Journal of Primary Prevention,* 12(2), 149–167.

Hall, R. E. (2008). Rooming in the master's house: Psychological domination and the black conservative. *Journal of Black Studies,* 38(4), 565–578.

Hardiman, R., and Jackson, B. W. (1997). Conceptual foundation for social justice courses. In M. Adams, L. A. Bell, and P. Griffin (Eds.), *Teaching for diversity and social justice: A sourcebook* (pp. 16–29). New York: Routledge.

Harrell, S. P. (2000). A multidimensional conceptualization of racism-related stress. *American Journal of Orthopsychiatry,* 70(1), 42–57.

Herek, G. M., Gillis, J. R., and Cogan, J. C. (1999). Psychological sequelae of hate crime victimization among lesbian, gay, and bisexual adults. *Journal of Consulting and Clinical Psychology,* 67(6), 945–951.

Jost, J. T., and Banaji, M. R. (1994). The role of stereotyping in system-justification and the production of false consciousness. *British Journal of Social Psychology,* 33, 1–27.

Jost, J., and Hunyady, O. (2002). The psychology of system justification and the palliative function of ideology. *European Review of Social Psychology,* 13, 111–153.

Kaiser, C. R. (2006). Dominant ideology threat and the interpersonal consequences of attributions to discrimination. In S. Levin and C. van Laar (Eds.), *Stigma and group Inequality: Social psychological perspectives* (pp. 45–64). Mahwah, NJ: Lawrence Erlbaum Associates.

Karlsen, S., and Nazroo, J. Y. (2002). Relation between racial discrimination, social class, and health among ethnic minority groups. *American Journal of Public Health,* 92(4), 624–631.

Keashly, L. (1998). Emotional abuse in the workplace: Conceptual and empirical issues. *Journal of Emotional Abuse,* 1(1), 85–117.

Klonoff, E. A., Landrine, H., and Ullman, J. B. (1999). Racial discrimination and psychiatric symptoms among blacks. *Cultural Diversity and Ethnic Minority Psychology,* 5(4), 329–339.

LaVan, H., and Martin, W. M. (2008). Bullying in the U.S. workplace: Normative and process-oriented ethical approaches. *Journal of Business Ethics,* 83(2), 147–165.

Lewis, R. J., Derlega, V. J., Clarke, E. G., and Kuang, J. C. (2006). Stigma consciousness, social constraints, and lesbian well-being. *Journal of Counseling Psychology,* 53(1), 48–56.

Lutgen-Sandvik, P., Namie, G., and Namie, R. (2009). Workplace bullying: Causes, consequences, and corrections. In P. Lutgen-Sandvik and B. D. Sypher (Eds.), *Destructive organizational communication: Processes, consequences, and constructive ways of organizing* (pp. 27–52). New York: Routledge.

Major, B. (2006). New perspectives on stigma and psychological well-being. In S. Levin and C. van Laar (Eds.), *Stigma and group inequality: Social psychological perspectives* (pp. 193–212). Mahwah, NJ: Lawrence Erlbaum Associates.

McAvoy, B. R., and Murtagh, J. (2003). Workplace bullying: The silent epidemic. *BMJ,* 326(7393), 776–777.

McLaughlin-Volpe, T. (2006). Understanding stigma from the perspective of the self-expansion model. In S. Levin and C. van Laar (Eds.), *Stigma and group inequality: Social psychological perspectives* (pp. 213–234). Mahwah, NJ: Lawrence Erlbaum Associates.

Mendoza-Denton, R., Page-Gould, E., and Pietrzak, J. (2006). Mechanisms for coping with status-based rejection expectations. In S. Levin and C. van Laar (Eds.), *Stigma and group inequality: Social psychological perspectives* (pp. 151–171). Mahwah, NJ: Lawrence Erlbaum Associates.

Metcalfe, J., and Mischel, W. (1999). A hot/cool-system analysis of delay of gratification: Dynamics of willpower. *Psychological Review,* 106(1), 3–19.

Meyer, I. H. (1995). Minority stress and mental health in gay men. *Journal of Health and Social Behavior,* 36(1), 38–56.

Meyer, I. H. (2003). Prejudice, social stress, and mental health in lesbian, gay, and bisexual populations. *Psychological Bulletin,* 129(5), 674–697.

Miller, C. T. (2006). Social psychological perspectives on coping with stressors related to stigma. In S. Levin and C. van Laar (Eds.), *Stigma and group inequality: Social psychological perspectives* (pp. 21–44). Mahwah, NJ: Lawrence Erlbaum Associates.

Myers, H. F., Lewis, T. T., and Parker-Dominguez, T. (2003). Stress, coping and minority health: Biopsychosocial perspective on ethnic health disparities. In G. Bernal, J. E. Trimble, A. K. Burlew, and F. T. L. Leong (Eds.), *Handbook of racial & ethnic minority psychology* (pp. 377–400). Thousand Oaks, CA: Sage Publications.

Park, L. E., and Crocker, J. (2008). Contingencies of self-worth and responses to negative interpersonal feedback. *Self & Identity,* 7(2), 184–203.

Pavalko, E. K., Mossakowski, K. N., and Hamilton, V. J. (2003). Does perceived discrimination affect health?: Longitudinal relationships between work discrimination and women's physical and emotional health. *Journal of Health and Social Behavior,* 44(1), 18–33.

Picca, L. H., and Feagin, J. (2007). *Two-faced racism: Whites in the backstage and frontstage.* New York: Routledge.

Pierce, C. M. (1995). Stress analogs of racism and sexism: Terrorism, torture, and disaster. In C. V. Willie, P. P. Rieker, B. M. Kramer, and B. S. Brown (Eds.), *Mental health, racism and sexism* (pp. 277–293). Pittsburgh, PA: University of Pittsburgh Press.

Poussaint, A. F. (1966). *The negro American: His self-image and integration.* Retrieved July 6, 2010, from http://www.ncbi.nlm.nih.gov/pmc/articles/PMC2611247/pdf/jnma005380053.pdf.

Poussaint, A. F., and Alexander, A. (2000). *Lay my burden down: Suicide and the mental health crisis among African Americans.* Boston: Beacon Press.

Prasad, P., Pringle, J. K., and Konrad, A. M. (2006). Examining the contours of workplace diversity: Concepts, contexts and challenges. In A. M. Konrad, P. Prasad, and J. K. Pringle (Eds.), *Handbook of workplace diversity* (pp. 1–22). Thousand Oaks, CA: Sage Publications.

Prilleltensky, I., and Gonick, L. S. (1994). The discourse of oppression in the social sciences: Past, present, and future. In E. J. Trickett, R. J. Watts, and D. Birman (Eds.), *Human diversity: Perspectives on people in context* (pp. 145–177). San Francisco: Jossey-Bass.

Ragins, B. R. (1997). Diversified mentoring relationships in organizations: A power perspective. *The Academy of Management Review,* 22(2), 482–521.

Ragins, B. R., Singh, R., and Cornwell, J. M. (2007). Making the invisible visible: Fear and disclosure of sexual orientation at work. *Journal of Applied Psychology,* 92(4), 1103–1118.

Ragins, B. R., and Sundstrom, E. (1989). Gender and power in organizations: A longitudinal perspective. *Psychological Bulletin,* 105(1), 51–88.

Rangasamy, J. (2004). Understanding institutional racism: Reflections from linguistic anthropology. In I. Law, D. Phillips, and L. Turney (Eds.), *Institutional racism in higher education* (pp. 27–34). Steerling, VA: Trentham Books.

Raver, J. L., and Nishii, L. H. (2010). Once, twice, or three times as harmful? Ethnic harassment, gender harassment, and generalized workplace harassment. *Journal of Applied Psychology,* 95(2), 236–254.

Rayner, C., and Hoel, H. (1997). A summary review of literature relating to workplace bullying. *Journal of Community & Applied Social Psychology,* 7, 181–191.

Rayner, C., Hoel, H., and Cooper, C. L. (2002). *Workplace bullying: What we know, who is to blame and what can we do?* New York: Taylor & Francis.

Roscigno, V. J. (2007). *The face of discrimination: How race and gender impact work and home lives.* Lanham, MD: Rowman & Littlefield.

Roscigno, V. J., Garcia, L. M., and Bobbitt-Zeher, D. (2007). Social closure and processes of race/sex employment discrimination. *The Annals of the American Academy of Political and Social Science,* 609(1), 16–48.

Roscigno, V. J., and Hodson, R. (2004). The organizational and social foundations of worker resistance. *American Sociological Review,* 69(1), 14–39.

Roscigno, V. J., Lopez, S. H., and Hodson, R. (2009). Supervisory bullying, status inequalities and organizational context. *Social Forces,* 87(3), 1561–1589.

Sanchez, F. J., and Vilain, F. (2009). Collective self-esteem as a coping resource for male-to-female transsexuals. *Journal of Counseling Psychology,* 56(1), 202–209.

Sapolsky, R. M. (1998). *Why zebras don't get ulcers: An updated guide to stress, stress-related diseases and coping* (2nd ed.). New York: W. H. Freeman.

Smith, R. A. (2002). Race, gender, and authority in the workplace: Theory and research. *Annual Review of Sociology,* 28, 509–542.

Swim, J. K., Hyers, L. L., Cohen, L. L., and Ferguson, M. J. (2001). Everyday sexism: Evidence for its incidence, nature, and psychological impact from three daily diary studies. *Journal of Social Issues,* 57(1), 31–53.

Swim, J. K., and Thomas, M. A. (2006). Responding to everyday discrimination: A synthesis of research on goal-directed, self-regulatory coping behaviors. In S. Levin and C. van Laar (Eds.), *Stigma and group inequality: Social psychological perspectives* (pp. 105–128). Mahwah, NJ: Lawrence Erlbaum Associates.

Szymanski, D. M. (2009). Examining potential moderators of the link between heterosexist events and gay and bisexual men's psychological distress. *Journal of Counseling Psychology,* 56(1), 142–151.

Tal, K. (1996). *Worlds of hurt: Reading the literatures of trauma.* New York: Cambridge University Press.

Thomas, R. R., Jr. (1990). From affirmative action to affirming diversity. *Harvard Business Review,* 90(2), 107–117.

Thompson, C. J., and Dey, E. L. (1998). Pushed to the margins: Sources of stress for African American college and university faculty. *Journal of Higher Education,* 69(3), 324–345.

Tierney, W. G. (2008). *The impact of culture on organizational decision-making: Theory and practice in higher education.* Steerling, VA: Stylus.

Twenge, J., and Crocker, J. (2002). Race, ethnicity, and self-esteem: Meta-analyses comparing Whites, Blacks, Hispanics, Asians, and Native Americans, including a commentary on Gray-Little and Hafdahl (2000). *Psychological Bulletin,* 128, 371–408.

Vega, W. A., and Rumbaut, R. G. (1991). Ethnic minorities and mental health. *Annual Review of Sociology,* 17, 351–383.

Waldo, C. R. (1999). Working in a majority context: A structural model of heterosexism as minority stress in the workplace. *Journal of Counseling Psychology,* 46(2), 218–232.

Waldron, V. (2009). Emotional tyranny at work: Suppressing the moral emotions. In P. Lutgen-Sandvik and B. D. Sypher (Eds.), *Destructive organizational communication: Processes, consequences, and constructive ways of organizing* (pp. 9–26). New York: Routledge.

Wei, M., Ku, T.-Y., Russell, D. W., Mallinckrodt, B., and Liao, K. Y.-H. (2008). Moderating effects of three coping strategies and self-esteem on perceived discrimination and depressive symptoms. *Journal of Counseling Psychology,* 55(4), 451–462.

Williams, D. R., Lavizzo-Mourey, R., and Warren, R. C. (1994). The concept of race and health status in America. *Public Health Reports,* 109(1), 26–41.

Williams, D. R., and Williams-Morris, R. (2000). Racism and mental health: The African American experience. *Ethnicity & Health,* 5(3/4), 243–268.

Williams, D. R., Yu, Y., Jackson, J. S., and Anderson, N. B. (1997). Racial differences in physical and mental health: Socio-economic status, stress and discrimination. *Journal of Health Psychology,* 2(3), 335–351.

Winant, H. (2004). *New politics of race: Globalism, difference, justice.* Minneapolis, MN: University of Minnesota Press.

Wornham, D. (2003). A descriptive investigation of morality and victimisation at work. *Journal of Business Ethics,* 45(1–2), 29–40.

Zuniga, X., Nagda, B. A., Chesler, M., and Cytron-Walker, A. (2007). *Intergroup dialogue in higher education: Meaningful learning about social justice.* San Francisco: Jossey-Bass.

3

ORGANIZATIONAL REALITIES AND ADMINISTRATIVE POWER STRUCTURES

> Discrimination, both sociologically and legally ... involves more than exclusion. It also entails differential treatment ... where the outcome is status hierarchy maintenance.
> —*Vincent J. Roscigno,* The Face of Discrimination, *2007, p. 10*

This chapter examines the *structural* and *contextual* components of the administrative environment that influence the level of equality in the workplace for university leadership on a daily basis. Structure and context are the channels that shape access to opportunity, resources, and career success. As proxies for mechanisms that vary across institutional settings, these components of organizational life reveal *how* variation is produced in ascriptive groups' differential access to opportunity, rather than *why* it occurs based upon gatekeepers' motives (Reskin, 2003). Agency plays an instrumental role in organizational inequality (Balser, 2002). We now focus upon the formal processes that allow such agency to shape career outcomes for diverse administrators. The "opportunity structure" for discrimination refers to structural conditions under which discrimination may be feasible and which, if employers discriminate, they would be most likely to succeed in the current legal environment (Petersen and Saporta, 2004).

Organizational and social processes underpin structural workplace elements and experiences and provide the medium through which social inequalities are reproduced. Given the difficulty of empirical verification of individual motives, organizational processes reveal the mechanisms through which motives can operate (Reskin, 2003). Key structural characteristics that govern these processes include leadership demographics, organizational design, reporting relationships, role-based attributes, institutional policies, and formal allocative processes of hiring, evaluation, promotion, compensation, discipline, and termination.

Since organizations represent "hothouses" that nurture status and power differences, power differentials enhance the ability of those in power to act upon stereotypes through contextual factors (Reskin, 2000). As a result, the controlled environment in the higher-education workplace represents a microcosm with its own rules—a kind of "total institution," or an enclosed world in which similarly situated individuals cut off from society at large lead an enclosed and formally administered life (Goffman, 1961). Every institution has encompassing characteristics and through these tendencies can be a forcing mechanism for changing persons (Goffman, 1961). Within the total institution, white normative practices are either implied or explicit, through the systems and processes that determine and define work existence (Feagin, 2006).

As we have seen from the narratives of diverse administrators, the pervasiveness, vast power, and resources of the total institution make resistance and challenge difficult at best. Deterrents to racism, sexism, and heterosexism may be weaker than institutional rhetoric implies, since individuals may not penalize the violation of egalitarian social norms due to the cognitive, emotional, and career costs of such protest (Kawakami, Dunn, Karmali, and Dovidio, 2009). As an arena of widely differentiated power, the temptation to exploit power is strong, especially when supervisors have unrestricted dominion that allows them to act like tyrants (Hodson, 2001). Managerial abuse can take shape in small, cumulative acts of humiliation and degradation that undermine individual dignity and competence.

Organizational processes are both relational and affiliative, with patterns of differential embeddedness in social networks substantially affecting access to support, sponsorship, training, tacit knowledge, and social capital (Vallas, 2003). Due to the importance of institutional assets in obtaining favorable treatment at work, lack of such resources affects the ability of diverse individuals to demonstrate competence and reinforces negative views by dominant group members (Vallas, 2003). Limitations to participation can include omission of diverse administrators from visible decision-making roles as well as opportunities to share their talents and perspectives in public, decision-making forums.

In this regard, Joan, the white administrator cited earlier, describes her surprise when she attended the meeting of a newly formed strategic university taskforce and noted the absence of minorities and the small number of women. As she explains, "... and there are about fifteen people there, and all but two are white males and the other two are white females. And our university is about 50 percent female and we are only about 10 percent minority, but it was very obvious to me."

This example illustrates how consciously or unconsciously administrators may be excluded from key decision-making groups as well as the prevailing context of white norms and rules. Remember the small town atmosphere where Joan's university is located and her observation that in this largely white community, minorities are less welcome. The omission of diverse participants from this taskforce could only reinforce the sense of isolation felt by disadvantaged group members and overlook important perspectives in the university's strategic efforts.

Returning to Mark's narrative, he similarly describes how he has not been invited to serve on key decision-making forums related to his position and his own uncertainty as to whether this exclusion is based upon the fact that he is Asian American or upon other factors:

> ... not being invited to meetings or, to serve, be on committees that my job should be considered for (not me personally), oh yeah, this happens quite often. And again my experience is that institutions have a certain set of people that they consider for particular decision making. And even though in my case my official position warrants my presence, I wasn't part of that group so it is very much an in-group/out-group situation. The out-group may be that I am a person of color or it may be something else.

And Megin, the white female administrator cited earlier, notes the informal types of exclusion from opportunities to comment or participate in decision-making meetings, despite her expertise in certain subject areas. She observes, "I think it is a matter of informal ... it's all informal.... It's meetings, and inviting people to comment, and not inviting others to comment, it's not even getting to the meeting, not even getting to the table, it's all those things I have experienced. Even though I may be an expert in a particular topic, I am excluded from the discussion, because I feel like, you know, I am a female. . . . "

As we shall see in this chapter, the formal and frequently opaque mechanisms of hiring, performance evaluation, compensation, promotion, and disciplinary sanctions can offer the opportunity for subjectivity and particularistic treatment. Research findings indicate that discrimination tends not to occur when actions would be recognized as motivated by racial bias, but occurs when behavior can be justified by other factors (Dovidio, Gaertner, Kawakami, and Hodson, 2002; Saucier and Miller, 2003). As a result, gatekeeping actors can readily adapt or develop subtle and nuanced rationalizations for acts of social closure. The process of eroding an administrator's credibility may begin with subtle attacks that cast doubt on the individual's professionalism, conduct, competency, or work ethic. In particular, the potential for subjectivity increases when soft skills such as interactional skills of teamwork, ability to fit in, and collaboration serve as justification for employment actions (Moss and Tilly, 1996). The accumulation of incursions upon the employment record through performance evaluation and related organizational processes can tarnish the administrator's reputation and provide ammunition for later, more severe employment outcomes.

In a salient example, Michael, a black Affirmative Action administrator, describes how his new white male supervisor did not value his experience and dismissed his expertise, despite his documented record of long and exemplary service at the university. Feeling that he was measured by a different standard, he underwent significant stress, noting that "in every decision, every transaction I had to perform better, be better." Similarly, the testimony of middle-class black Americans in a ground-breaking study involving 209 interviews with African Americans underscores the reality that no amount of achievement or hard work, or even money, resources, or success can protect black individuals from the persistent incursions of white racism in their everyday lives (Feagin and Sikes, 1994).

The lack of support from Michael's new supervisor eventually led to Michael's retirement from the university. The separate but unequal gauntlet of administrative hurdles faced by this employee led to the loss of a talented and dedicated member of the university community who was responsible for safeguarding equal opportunity.

As a corollary to this avenue of inquiry, in this chapter we shall also explore the impact of the process of collusion upon organizational outcomes, both from the perspective of targeted individuals as well as bystanders from disadvantaged groups. When stigmatized groups engage in forms of self-oppression and denial of the existence of systemic discrimination, this defense of the system keeps the patriarchal, sexist, and heterosexist frame in play. And, in addition, collusion can benefit those who buy into the dominant ideology and even serve as spokespersons for this perspective.

To begin the discussion, we focus upon foundational elements of the power structure at the research university and examine how these elements can operate in tandem to reinforce existing patterns of social stratification. As we have seen, despite some gains by women and minorities in administrative positions, the dominance of white males in leadership positions in the university continues to support a socially stratified hierarchy. Maintenance of the status quo alone is sufficient to perpetuate existing racial stratification (Smith and Elliott, 2002).

The Demographics and Design of Leadership

How do the demographics of leadership in the research university affect the distribution and dynamics of power? Large organizations contain within themselves an internal power struggle among leading protagonists in terms of control of the goals and resources of the organization based upon formal authority and ownership (Fligstein, 1987). The bases of power must be structural, rather than personal (Fligstein, 1987). The typical university organizational structure is composed of the following principal positions reporting to the president or an executive vice president: provost (overseeing Academic Affairs including deans and department chairs); vice president or chief enrollment officer for student affairs; chief financial officer (CFO); chief information officer (CIO); and vice president for university advancement. More recently, additional executive positions may include a vice president for research, a chief diversity officer (CDO), and a chief human resources officer (CHRO).

The structure of higher education is strikingly white-male dominated with close to 85 percent of the top-ranked positions in doctorate-granting institutions held by whites and 66 percent held by males (King and Gomez, 2008). The only exception to this pattern of white-male dominance is the Chief Diversity Officer position which is held by 12.3 percent white incumbents, while 70.8 percent of these positions are held by African Americans (King and Gomez, 2008). Table 3.1 addresses the demographics of senior administrators in doctorate-granting institutions.

Table 3.1 Characteristics of Senior Administrators: Doctorate-granting Institutions

	Chief of Staff (%)	Executive Vice President (%)	CAO/ Provost (%)	Central Senior Academic Affairs Officer (%)	Dean of Academic College (%)	Senior Administrative Officer (%)	Senior External Affairs Officer (%)	Senior Student Affairs Officer (%)	Chief Diversity Officer (%)	Total (%)
Race/Ethnicity										
White	83.2	95.8	93.3	87.1	86.2	87.4	86.9	77.2	12.3	84.2
Gender										
Female	61.6	16.0	23.0	37.1	19.3	37.8	34.6	38.5	56.1	34.0
Male	38.4	84.0	77.0	62.9	80.7	62.2	65.4	61.5	43.9	66.0

Source: King & Gomez, 2008.

Chief Academic Affairs Officers

At most institutions, Chief Academic Officers or Provosts are considered as second in line to the presidency and this position is the typical pathway to the presidency. Chief Academic Officers (CAOs) on average remain only 4.7 years in an institution, less than half the length of the average presidential tenure (Mann, 2010). Chief Academic Officers are predominantly white males (85 percent), with women comprising 32 percent of CAOs at doctorate-granting institutions ("ACE Releases First National Census," 2010). A study conducted by Eduventures Academic Leadership Learning Collaborative of 323 CAOs found the three most common reasons for departure were expanded job responsibilities without accompanying resources (50 percent), financial issues at the institution (50 percent) and faculty discontent (30 percent). As a result, 40 percent said that the job had become less desirable (Mann, 2010).

Chief Student Affairs Officers

In higher education, the diversity of leadership roles varies significantly by major functional area, with greater diversity in Student Affairs leadership roles (22.8 percent) compared to Academic Affairs, Finance, and Technology leadership positions. An increased percentage of student affairs leaders in doctorate-granting institutions are African American (15.5 percent), a trend with important effects on African American student engagement (Jackson, 2003; King and Gomez, 2008). Given the growing enrollment of African American students in predominantly white institutions (PWIs), student experiences, contact, and development must be considered in terms of a supportive representative bureaucracy (Flowers, 2003; Jackson, 2003; Jackson and O'Callaghan, 2009). In other words, the greater the diversity of a constituent group, the more diversity that is required of the leaders making policy decisions on behalf of the group (Flowers, 2003).

Chief Information Officers

The Chief Information Officer (CIO) position is a traditionally white–male dominated occupation, with women in higher education representing slightly over one-fourth of technology leaders (Brown, 2008). Although the CIO position has existed for about twenty-five years, the career path is not as well-defined in higher education as the Chief Financial Officer and has taken longer to become standardized (Brown, 2009). In fact, one survey indicates that the Chief Financial Officer oversees the technology area in 23 percent of the higher-education institutions responding, with only 39 percent reporting to the Chief Executive Officer (Brown, 2008).

Perhaps no other role in higher education has undergone so much change, and given the familiarity and expansion of computing knowledge, some institutions such as the Massachusetts Institute of Technology and the University of Chicago have downgraded their top technology positions (Young, 2010). If the CIO position is seen as more operational than strategic, then it will be less likely to contribute at the cabinet-level table (Young, 2010). Diversity in this executive-level position is still extremely limited, but tenure in the CIO position often involves longer tenure than other positions (six years and seven months) (Brown, 2008).

The Dominance of the Chief Financial Officer in Nonacademic Administration

While the primary focus of Chief Financial Officers (CFOs) is upon financial administration, the prominence of the financial officer position in university administration has increased. With the dwindling of external resources and rising enrollment challenges, funding and budget issues have taken center stage at the university. The rise of the CFO can be seen in the increased involvement of the CIO in institutional strategy across multiple divisions and in control of the distribution of resources. Chief Financial Officers wield considerable power and influence not only due to their oversight of financial areas but also due to their widening span of influence in nonacademic administration and strategic decision making. More than two-thirds have responsibilities for facilities, auxiliary services, and human resources, while more than half oversee public safety, internal audit, and endowment (National Association of University Business Officers, 2010). Some also oversee the information technology function.

A survey of 974 Chief Financial Officers found the typical CFO to be a fifty-five-year-old white male who has been in his position about seven years (National Association of University Business Officers, 2010). In fact, at comprehensive universities just 21 percent of CFOs are women (National Association of University Business Officers, 2010). The following tables compare the gender, race, and ethnicity of CFOs with Chief Academic Officers (CAOs) based on the 2008 Survey of Chief Academic Officers conducted by the American Council of Education (National Association of University Business Officers, 2010). Despite the increasing diversification of student enrollment, the two most powerful administrative roles under the president are still largely held by white males, as shown in Tables 3.2 and 3.3.

More than 80 percent of CFOs at comprehensive and research universities attained their positions from within higher education, due to good promotional prospects for promotion from lower-level positions (National Association of University Business Officers, 2010). Women, however, are more likely to attain the CFO position as a lateral move between institutions, rather than as an internal promotional opportunity (National Association of University Business Officers, 2010). These statistics tend to suggest heightened advantage for internal promotion for men in the financial area.

Richard Eckman, President of the Council of Independent Colleges, notes the increase in vice presidents in nonacademic areas such as finance, development, and enrollment (23 percent overall) (Ekman, 2010). He suggests college leadership is in imminent crisis when the enterprise is run by individuals who have never served in academic roles, and may view education as a production problem that must be solved efficiently or a brand to be marketed (Ekman, 2010). The focus upon efficiency has given the CFO role increased prominence, visibility, and influence, particularly with the consolidation of a broad array of nonacademic functions.

Table 3.2 Distribution of CFOs and CAOs by Gender

Gender	CFOs	CAOs
Male	68%	60%
Female	32%	40%

Source: King and Gomez, 2008.

Table 3.3 Distribution of CFOs and CAOs by Race

Race/Ethnicity	CFOs	CAOs
White, Non-Hispanic	90%	85%
Black/African American	5%	6%
Hispanic/Latino	—	4%
Asian/Pacific Islander	3%	2%
American Indian	—	1%
Other*	2%	1%

Source: National Association of University Business Officers, 2010, p.11.

The Reporting Relationship of Human Resources and its Policy Role

Significant research underscores the value of cohesive human resource systems, policies, and operations to organizational success, financial results, and competitive advantage (see, for example, Ulrich, 1997; Ulrich, Allen, Brockbank, Younger, and Nyman, 2009; Ulrich and Smallwood, 2003). From a theoretical perspective, human resource practices that minimize bias in personnel decisions and require objective and reliable information should serve as a curb to discriminatory practices (Reskin, 2000, 2003). Nonetheless, several factors can diminish or neutralize the impact of human resource safeguards: 1) the secondary organizational position of human resources in many universities; 2) the political pressures exerted upon the department due to this secondary role; and 3) the lack of awareness and/or recognition by human resource and equal opportunity practitioners of the nature and prevalence of subtle discrimination.

While a small proportion of educational institutions have established a Chief Human Resource Officer reporting to the CEO of a system (2.1 percent) or to the President of a single institution (19.6 percent), more than half of all Chief Human Resource Officers (57.9 percent) report through the Chief Business Officer (34.4 percent), the Chief Financial Officer (14.2 percent), or the Chief Administration Officer (9.3 percent) (CUPA Administrative Compensation Survey, 2009–2010). From an organizational perspective, the lack of authority and secondary position of Human Resources under the financial area limits the authority and independence of the department in reviewing institutional decisions and in strategic contributions to decision-making processes. Table 3.4 identifies the reporting relationships of Chief Human Resource Officers.

In addition, the demographic composition of Chief Human Resource Officers reflects greater diversity than Chief Financial Officers, with 66.6 percent females and 15.5 percent minorities. The feminization of the human-resource role is a predominant trend, with most women human resource officers reporting to male CFOs. The university has been slow to realize the importance of bringing the human-resources voice to the executive leadership table to foster more inclusive talent management strategies. We have seen the lack of diversity in decision-making positions at the Cabinet level except in the role of Chief Diversity Officer. Consonant with the findings of Collins' study of seventy-six black corporate executives cited earlier, minority leaders

Table 3.4 Reporting Relationships of Chief Human Resource Officers

Title	2009–2010	
CEO of a System or District	24	2.1%
CEO of a Single Institution	220	19.6%
Executive Vice President	90	8.0%
Chief Academic Officer and Provost	9	0.8%
Chief Business Officer	386	34.4%
Chief Administration Officer	104	9.3%
Chief Financial Officer	159	14.2%
Other	129	11.5%
No Response	159	
Valid Total	1,121	100.0%
Overall Total	1,280	

Source: College and University Professional Association for Human Resources, 2010.

in university administration may be tracked into staff not line positions, with high-ranking titles but little actual power, that are frequently focused on diversity, equity, or affirmative action, (Collins, 1997). The role of human resources in addressing these trends will require support from the President to ensure that women, minorities, and LGBT administrators attain genuine authority and actual decision-making power in their roles.

The Influence of Supervisory-Subordinate Demography on Job Success

Given existing patterns of social stratification in the administrative ranks of the university, we now turn to an examination of the impact of relational demography on supervisor-subordinate relationships. What are the dynamics when diverse administrators assume the role of supervisors over majority staff members and vice versa? How do ascriptive similarity and dissimilarity in the supervisory-subordinate dyad affect opportunity, job satisfaction, and well-being for members of traditionally disadvantaged groups?

As we have seen from the demographic analysis of university leadership, the bureaucratic structure of the university is led by a group of elite white men, and the infrastructure of the workplace is established, normed, and framed by this predominantly white, male, heterosexist perspective. Yet the influence of relational demography upon career success has received almost no acknowledgment or attention within the research university.

The demography of the supervisor-subordinate relationship is a pivotal factor in the job success of upper-level administrators, as supported through research findings and the interview narratives. Over the last two decades, an emerging body of research has probed the explanatory potential of relational demography in relation to workplace outcomes, supporting the proposition that those in power prefer others like themselves (see for example, Baldi and McBrier, 1997; Elliott and Smith, 2004; James, 2000; Landau, 1995; Moss and Tilly, 1996; Smith, 2002; Smith, 2005; Smith and Elliott, 2002; Tsui and O'Reilly, 1989; Wesolowski and Mossholder, 1997).

Since whites are the primary decision makers, they benefit most from in-group preference, and have a stake in developing and sustaining job segregation by sifting minorities with equivalent human capital into lower-ranking positions (Elliott and Smith, 2001). Non-white, non-male individuals must conform to the existing system that reproduces its essential features as white, male, and heterosexist. The similarity-attraction paradigm or the concept of "coethnic reproduction" refers to the process through which powerful organizational decision makers tend to promote members of their own racial or ethnic group to supervisory positions under them and exclude or limit minority members from gaining access to power (Smith and Elliott, 2002). The intertwining of race and gender has been less studied, but research indicates that race and gender stratification are not mutually exclusive networks: they overlap to produce different outcomes for different groups (Elliott and Smith, 2004; Smith, 2005).

Rosabeth Kanter's concept of "homosocial reproduction" in her pioneering work *Men and Women of the Corporation* (1977) identified the "uncertainty quotient" or the relationship between the increasing need for increased trust and discretion in upper-level positions and a tendency to select similar others (Kanter, 1977). The impact of demographic difference intensifies at higher levels of the organization as job responsibilities become more consequential, amorphous, and non-routine, resulting in subjective assessments that may reflect similarity to self or commonalities in background rather than requisite skills (Elliott and Smith, 2001; Johnsrud and Heck, 1994). The replicative process of homosocial reproduction can have significant consequences for the careers of minorities, women, and LGBT administrators. For example, a comprehensive study based upon data from a multi-city urban survey that found that white men were twice as likely to be promoted to manager when overseen by a white male supervisor than when overseen by an ascriptively dissimilar supervisor (Elliott and Smith, 2004).

Similarity and in-group preference affect frequency of communication and frequency of interaction in work settings, factors that can be determinative for work outcomes (see Tsui and O'Reilly, 1989, for review). In this regard, a study of 296 employees in two firms revealed that the racial composition of supervisor-subordinate relationships was linked to job satisfaction and perceptions of procedural justice, increasing the sensitivity of subordinates about exchanges with their supervisors (Wesolowski and Mossholder, 1997). Interestingly, a study of 344 managers found a preference by superiors for subordinates who were younger, less educated, and with shorter job tenure, a phenomenon that may reflect the supervisors' need for psychological comfort in terms of confidence and power (Tsui and O'Reilly, 1989).

The concept of the "sticky floor" versus the "glass ceiling" suggests that group composition influences authority attainment: ethnic groups concentrated at entry levels will restrict authority chances for ethnic minorities and dominance of minority groups at higher levels increase the chances of authority gain (Smith and Elliott, 2002). Another study based upon 4,390 employees in a multi-city urban dataset revealed that white men working in occupational niches dominated by whites are more likely to hold positions of authority, whereas the odds of black women holding positions of high authority were less than half those of white females (Smith and Elliott, 2002). Black men were either concentrated in positions of low authority or high authority in a seemingly all-or-nothing proposition, whereas Asian men were nearly as likely as white men to hold positions of authority (Smith and Elliott, 2002).

Blocked opportunity through the structural characteristics of the workplace is linked to the negative psychosocial consequences of institutional discrimination, as demonstrated in a study based upon two major surveys (Forman, 2003). The data reveals that racial segmentation in the workplace negatively impacted African Americans' psychological well-being and sense of control over their lives, particularly among higher-status blacks (Forman, 2003). Furthermore, when African Americans perceived their current position as a "black position," these individuals experienced decreased levels of life satisfaction and increased levels of psychological distress (Forman, 2003).

Perhaps less well-understood is the difficulty minority, women, and LGBT supervisors may encounter when overseeing ascriptively different subordinates. In particular, the notion of two tournaments applies to diverse administrators in the process of garnering the respect and authority associated with a high-level position from predominantly majority staffs. Female supervisors encounter the incongruity of male and female social roles that creates a "double bind" when they are expected to be assertive and even forceful, whereas female stereotypes suggest cooperation and interpersonal attributes (see Schieman and McMullen, 2008, for review).

For example, two different white male CEOs in a survey of fifteen Fortune 500 companies described women of color as either not aggressive enough or as too aggressive and trying too hard (Giscombe and Mattis, 2002). Minority supervisors can be characterized as nasty, tyrannical, or controlling when they take actions that would be characterized as effective and strong when enacted by white males. The dynamics of these interactions may affect the level of instrumental support diverse leaders receive from their staffs as well as their ability to create a unified team. In addition, the impact of LGBT supervisors on predominantly heterosexual staffs has received little, if any, research attention.

Elite white men are, by intention, the deciding actors in the university workplace, and determine career outcomes for diverse administrators. This relational demography is a prime characteristic of the supervisory-subordinate relationship and affects opportunities, choices, and instrumental support for diverse administrators at the highest levels of the university. Yet despite the existence of a significant body of research in this regard, universities have not begun to address demographic issues of context and structure as a matter of policy or practice, and instead have adopted a meritocratic, "color-blind," and "diversity-blind" approach to employment outcomes.

Hiring

While hiring is the gateway to increased administrative diversity at the university, little is known about how screening and selection processes actually unfold. In comparison with their white counterparts ($M=2.92$, $SD=1.230$), African American and black administrators in this study felt minorities have difficulty in attaining desirable jobs and incomes relative to their white counterparts ($M=4.23$, $SD=.725$), $t(35.81)=-4.163$, $p<.001$. Although the hiring process offers great opportunity for bias through the weight of subjective assessments, it is hardly studied and poorly understood due to the difficulty of assembling the relevant data on both the applicant and employer sides (Petersen, Saporta, and Seidel, 2000).

Screening and search processes for upper-level administration are often handled by executive search firms, adding an additional layer of complexity.

Due to the fact that executive search processes typically elude the level of scrutiny of a completely campus-based search, the level of transparency varies considerably. Search firms send out announcements to qualified candidates and stakeholders, soliciting applications and nominations. They conduct screening processes that determine which candidates are invited for on-campus interviews by a search committee, and prepare extensive analyses of references and background information.

The processes by which executive search firms evaluate diverse candidates for upper-level university positions are a subject that will benefit from further research exploration. Some search firms maintain a high degree of rigor in how they screen candidates, while others may appear to use less rigorous methodology as they attempt to find candidates who do not represent a risk to the firm's advocacy. Such methods often seek to eliminate candidates with any flaws in their background or to delve for information using more subjective means. Yet the more formal the methods, the more women and minorities may benefit, given the opportunity to document credentials, skills, and experience, rather than through more subjective information that occurs in informal methods (Drentea, 1998).

A second consideration in administrative appointments is the "wired search" in which an internal candidate is preselected, a mechanism that preserves the advantages of white males in many organizations (Bielby, 2000). While the position may be publicly advertised, an internal candidate has been identified, and position qualifications may be altered to reflect that candidate's particular background.

In the hiring process itself, the evaluation of candidates can involve considerable subjectivity. Of particular relevance is a study that found that when qualifications for a given position were less obvious and the decision involved more ambiguity, white participants recommended black candidates less frequently than white candidates (45 percent versus 76 percent) with the same credentials (Dovidio and Gaertner, 2000; Dovidio, Gaertner, Kawakami, and Hodson, 2002 for review). The benefit of the doubt that was extended to white candidates was not similarly extended to minority candidates (Dovidio and Gaertner, 2000; Dovidio, Gaertner, Kawakami, and Hodson, 2002). Black or minority candidates may be hired as tokens or, as an administrator and professor in a Black Studies program in a predominantly white university commented, "They're paying you as administrators to stay in line and help them. In that case, you're kind of a fire insurance against black people" (Feagin and Sikes, 1994, p. 159).

In negotiating the final salary offer, a study of over 3,000 salary offers in a high-technology company found that minority group members negotiated significantly lower salaries than majority individuals, although this effect was reduced when they had internal social ties within the organization (Seidel, Polzer, and Stewart, 2000). Minority group members, were, however, less likely to have such internal social ties to the organization that would mitigate this outcome.

Due to the fact that criteria for high-level positions may be viewed as impossible to measure systematically, minimizing bias in the selection process is especially difficult (Bielby, 2000). Men may have greater access to newly created positions that are tailored to their individual backgrounds and interests (Drentea, 2000). As a result, pre-selection and wiring of searches intensify the potential for selecting candidates through the similarity-attraction paradigm that favors white males at higher echelons of the administrative hierarchy, rather than based upon strict comparative evaluation of qualifications.

Promotion, Advancement, and Compensation

Is the process of attainment of institutional rewards such as promotion and compensation the same for all demographic groups? Promotional opportunities and expansion of an individual's scope of responsibility may be the new battleground for equalizing opportunities, since research indicates that different models of advancement pertain to different disadvantaged groups (Elliott and Smith, 2004).

Several prominent studies identify different tracks of advancement for minorities and women than for white males. For example, an extensive study based on the Multi-City Survey of Urban Inequality (MCSUI) concluded that in comparison with white men, different groups are disadvantaged for different reasons in different ways (Smith, 2005). Although the study did not reveal differences in promotion rates or network sponsorship, process differences leading to promotion varied for minority men and women (Smith, 2005). Specifically, minority men and women needed to accrue more time-dependent factors including total work experience, years with current employer, and job-specific experience to be promoted (Smith, 2005). This evidence implies that minority men and women's performance attributes are placed under greater scrutiny, and more time and energy are needed for minorities and women to build relationships of trust with supervisors before promotion can occur (Smith, 2005).

Another study of 396 employees found that black workers with comparable education, training, and experience in similar types of firms were only half as likely as their white counterparts to be promoted, while male workers were twice as likely as their female counterparts to be promoted (Baldi and McBrier, 1997). The study concluded that race-specific models of promotion differ within a sample of U.S. firms, with formal criteria for promotion such as education less likely to be applied to whites than blacks (Baldi and McBrier, 1997). In fact, sponsorship models for whites based upon personal ties and informal relationships may prevail as opposed to a contest model for blacks (Baldi and McBrier, 1997). And a study of 127 managers in a firm in the financial service industry found race to have an effect on promotion rates and psychosocial support (James, 2000). The findings inferred that blacks experience treatment discrimination in the nature and influence of workplace relationships, with fewer strong ties and a less valuable network (James, 2000). In addition, human capital investments such as additional training had differential benefits, enhancing the promotability of white managers but not black managers (James, 2000).

An analysis of the career paths of fifty-four executives and managers in three corporations also found the existence of two tournaments with separate rules for white and black executives and managers (Thomas and Gabarro, 1999). The tax of time affected the early career paths of minority executives, suggesting that the criteria governing promotion are more rigorous for minorities, involving a longer proving period and greater scrutiny (Thomas and Gabarro, 1999).

To illustrate how the road to advancement can vary based upon ascriptive characteristics in higher-education administration, we turn to the account of Julie, a white female administrator in a large research university. Julie shares how gender-based inequity affected her opportunity for advancement within a male-dominated environment, despite comparable education and human capital investments. Throughout several years of employment, Julie discussed with her supervisor the observed pay differentials between herself and her male counterparts. Each year, she was told that, in order to earn a raise, she must meet certain goals. When those goals were met, she was told to wait yet another year, and given other goals to prove herself.

During that time period, Julie enrolled in a doctoral program. As she pursued her doctorate, she repeatedly had conversations with her supervisor regarding her interest in obtaining a higher position or adjusted title once the degree was completed. Upon completion of the degree, she once again approached her supervisor. Since he was no longer her direct supervisor, he suggested that she begin a discussion with the dean. Julie describes her attempts to meet with the dean: "I put together a ... proposal and I sent it to my ... supervisor in preparation of our meeting and suggested that I be an assistant dean since that's more again similar to what other people who are on campus, I believe they are all male ... my counterparts ... I ... got a meeting with him, but then he quickly cancelled it and when I tried to reschedule it, he wouldn't call me and wouldn't honor my emails." Eventually, the dean finally agreed to speak with Julie about her proposal, but would not agree to meet face-to-face. During the telephone discussion, the dean made it very clear that Julie's proposal would not be given serious consideration. Julie continues:

> [The dean] ... said to me, 'Look I am not even going to read your proposal ... I will tell you this right now; you have no future in this school.... You have no future career here.' In other words, I am fine where I am ... but don't expect to be promoted at all. And I asked why and he said ... , 'Well let me tell you a story.' And he brought up this other female employee that had worked in the environment and basically the point of the story was that she got too big for her britches and she didn't work out.... So in other words, he was clearly sending me a message, there is a finite place for a woman here and you are trying to overstep that.... I kept saying ... I don't want money ... all I am trying to make it equitable compared to what my colleagues across campus who have much less responsibility.... I am simply trying to level that playing field, and he said no....

After a number of years in her position, despite her many contributions to the organization, Julie felt devalued and helpless. Although she was clearly aware of hushed talk about the existence of an "old-boys' network," this was the first time that she directly experienced the limitations of her gender within the environment. She articulates her reaction to the dean's statements in these words: "... you're fine as long as you know your place, and as long as you can do what I need you to do, but there is never a sense of recognition, there is never a sense of opportunity, promotion, valuing. As a matter of fact ... he (the dean) teased me a little bit ... he did tell me that my degree ... was basically useless in that school, and that I needed to be in ... another field...."

Similarly, research findings indicate that advancement in compensation may take different paths for different disadvantaged groups. In this regard, a major study compared job authority and income among black and white respondents at three levels of authority over a twenty-two year period between

1972 and 1994, using data from the National Opinion Research Center's General Social Survey (Smith, 1997). The study substantiated a glass-ceiling effect for black men who earn less than white men, even after adjusting for occupational position, human capital attributes, and other factors, with no sign that this differential return in relation to authority changed between 1972 and 1994 (Smith, 1997). The compensation gap was greatest among men in the highest-level positions and actually increased over time, validating the fact that "race continues to be an enduring, determinative factor in black men's life chances" (Smith, 1997, p. 34). Another study based upon a large Fortune 500 company and a sample of 2,699 supervisors and 32,854 subordinates found support for the congruence of the ethnicity of subordinates and supervisors in terms of higher salaries when the pay system is merit-based, presumably allowing for variation in supervisor recommendations (Avey, West, and Crossley, 2008).

Despite the fact that large organizations including universities are subject to outside scrutiny in response to Equal Employment Opportunity and Affirmative Action laws and regulations, efforts to advance women and minorities may be symbolic rather than substantive, and represent simply "going through the motions" without real impact on internal barriers (Bielby, 2000). As shown by research findings, substantive barriers to advancement pertain to disadvantaged groups including greater scrutiny of accomplishments, the need for more significant human capital investments than majority counterparts to be considered for expanded roles, and increased investments of time and energy to sustain their positions.

The Nexus between Formal and Informal Performance Evaluation

Performance appraisal is a particularly influential indicator that reveals *how* the dynamics of subtle discrimination unfold, since it represents the official institutional evaluation of job performance. In this regard, field and laboratory studies indicate that biases increase as evaluation criteria become more subjective as members of disadvantaged groups approach higher status positions (see Dovidio and Gaertner, 1996 for review). Such hidden or unconscious biases may be more intensely manifested in situations where whites are either directly or symbolically threatened by the advancement of underrepresented groups to positions of control and status and seek to maintain the status quo

(Dovidio and Gaertner, 1996). And the greater the uncertainty or difficulty associated with evaluating performance or competence, the stronger the likelihood that social similarity will be used as a proxy and the more significant the impact of biases and attributions (see Ibarra, 1993, for review).

A number of large-scale research studies have documented disparities in performance ratings for black and white employees, with considerably lower ratings for blacks (see, for example, Landau, 1995; Lefkowitz and Battista, 1995; Sackett and Dubois, 1991; Sackett, Dubois, and Noe, 1991). One study of 1,628 managers and their supervisors in three companies that reports more negative organizational experiences for blacks partially attributes the lower ratings received by black managers to less job discretion and lower feelings of acceptance (Greenhaus, Parasuraman, and Wormley, 1990). Similarly, analyses of male-versus-female performance evaluations in a study of 489 upper-middle and senior-level positions found evidence that women holding line positions were assessed more stringently than men as well as than other women in staff positions and held to a stricter standard for promotion (Lyness and Heilman, 2006). Since typically line positions have greater organizational authority and influence, the incongruity of stereotypes attributed to women (as kind, relationship-oriented, and nurturing) versus those ascribed to men (as achievement-oriented, tough, and forceful) give rise to a lack-of-fit model in terms of fulfilling job expectations that is reflected in performance evaluations (Lyness and Heilman, 2006).

While performance evaluations are meant to provide a continuous process of feedback and coaching as well as objective identification of goals and areas of improvement, the evaluation can instead serve as the crystallization of a number of informal factors and observations as we see in the following example shared by Therese, an African American female administrator in a prestigious university. She describes how informal evaluation of an African American female colleague's style resulted in the administrator being managed out of the university. Therese speculates that her colleague's white female supervisor did not communicate her expectations to her colleague, perhaps due to fear of being termed a racist. She identifies the factors that she believes led to her colleague's departure:

> ... it was clear that no one had sat down and had a discussion with individuals about their expectations. And the expectations were changing and then there was a lot of scrutiny around everything this person—actually this has happened to a number of people that I have known in my organization—in fear of, you know, of being called like a racist, or you know, having bias,

they never had taken the time to have a communication about the expectations rather it was, you know, what someone wore or how they conducted themselves or what they did. And so then everything had come under scrutiny and it became unbearable for the person to actually maintain their employment so they resigned...

Instead of someone you know, saying, well, you know, we are pretty stuffy around here, we tend to be a little more conservative ... I would suggest that you wear skirts that, you know, are longer than the ones that you currently wear, because of whatever. And so not saying anything, everything is scrutinized from her work. It was a culmination of those things. She was hired for a certain level of expertise. And because her style was different, everything she did was ... evaluated in very subjective ways.

There is no policy on, you know, the types of things you can have in your office. She brought in some things which seemed reasonable for ... things to have in the office. She brought in her personal water cooler; I mean she paid for it, you know, brought the five-gallon water jugs in or she had them delivered which was certainly appropriate. But then there was no discussion on ... did this go too far, which is very subjective, there was no clear policy on the things that you can hang on your wall or things you can bring into the office to make the space yours.

They criticized the way she personalized her office. And she had some things, some items that you could consider black art or African art, she had all of her college degrees posted, hung on her wall ... and she had a water cooler in her office. ... I am not sure it actually made it to her written evaluation, but that was the type of things that would be evaluated. She didn't check in with anyone to see if it was appropriate and that was the thing against her. ... So then all of those things had come into play on her originality and a team player ... and all those things that come under that umbrella and she began to be managed out of the organization.

Despite the university's elevated reputation for scholarly excellence, Therese's narrative indicates the prevalence of what one researcher terms "a discriminatory work culture" in which dominant group members perceive, judge, and enforce behavioral boundaries on a day-to-day basis, requiring minorities and women to signal that they really do fit in (Green, 2005). These daily inequities exert their damaging force by walling out the person of difference and making the individual less effective (Rowe, 2008).

In other ways, the subtle language of evaluation may be fine-tuned to provide an aura of objectivity while understating accomplishments, providing undocumented critical comments, and even casting doubt upon the diverse administrator's professionalism, competence, abilities, and conduct. Assessments of soft skills are "inevitably subjective," providing the opportunity for discrimination to enter such assessments (Moss and Tilly, 1996).

Laying the Groundwork: Disciplinary and Layoff Processes

Disciplinary and layoff processes can serve as a prelude or actual gateway to acts of employment closure, and create a perilous situation for diverse administrators, even in the face of positive performance evaluations and objective accomplishments. The concept of discipline is generally contradictory to the expectations for administrative positions, since most administrators are at will employees, who can be terminated without cause, unless protected by an employment contract. Nonetheless, disciplinary-type memoranda or other related disciplinary actions can be used to document the employment record to diffuse the potential for litigation.

Returning to Julie's narrative, she shares how an investigation differentially targeted her through the power and impact of the "old boy" network in her university. Changes in upper administration directly impacted Julie's standing within the organization. An employee with a solid employment record for many years, Julie had received accolades for her effectiveness in operating her department and positive performance evaluations. When forced by her supervisor to hire the family member of an influential white male administrator in order to earn the influential administrator's favor, Julie expressed concern over the political implications if the employee did not work out. Julie was assured that no harm would come to her should she need to terminate the employee.

During the first several months of the new employee's tenure, the upper administration underwent change. Upon termination of the employee, the incoming supervisor was advised by a colleague of Julie's (who had a documented history of bullying Julie and had a vested interest in keeping the favor of the influential administrator) to investigate Julie's department, as it had a "history of problems." Without any discussion or direct communication with Julie, the incoming supervisor sanctioned an unorthodox and secretive investigation of the department, creating an atmosphere of fear and distrust. The investigatory questions were framed to solicit negative feedback, despite the fact that there were no prior indications of problems. Julie explains the way questions were asked of all her staff: "'We understand that there are a lot of concerns [within your department] ... we want to hear them; we want to know what is wrong; we want to know what your frustrations are.' They never asked anything ... never said, 'Please tell us your experience; please tell us things, let us know how things are going? Please tell us the pluses and minuses.'" The findings of the investigation, which were not aligned with any expectations previously communicated to Julie, were used by management to proceed with disciplinary action against Julie.

This example powerfully illustrates how disciplinary processes can provide the opportunity structure and channel for the exercise of particularistic agendas. In contrast to the treatment she received, Julie indicates that a male colleague who displayed sexist behavior toward Julie, called her a "lazy bitch," and yelled and banged his fists in meetings was rewarded with a promotion. As Julie explains,

> The same types of things that I don't do in an aggressive manner, men do, men are very aggressive here, and I don't do things in an aggressive manner, so I feel like I am not being heard. And I have constantly been told basically to be one of the boys.... That kind of behavior is very valued here ... it [is] very much male, aggressive type of behavior that [gets] rewarded. And so every time he'd yell and shout and bang his fists, it got more positive attention.... So I feel that again those kinds of behaviors are continuing to be rewarded.

The findings of the investigation of Julie's managerial style surfaced only in typical staff complaints in relation to supervisory style, yet still resulted in documented expectations that Julie and her all-female management team give more kudos and rewards, positive strokes, and interpersonal time to the staff members. By contrast, while her male colleague continued to be rewarded for aggressive behavior, Julie was held to a different set of expected behaviors that could be considered traditionally female characteristics.

In another example, Christine, the white female lesbian administrator cited earlier, recalls the differential application of disciplinary standards to her by a new supervisor in her labor-relations role. This incident took place at an earlier time in her career when she had not yet come out of the closet. She had recently completed her law degree and taken a demotion to learn the practice of labor relations under the tutelage of a supportive supervisor. When, however, her supervisor passed away, the new director applied sanctions without warning, contrary to established employee relations practice.

Christine believes the treatment she received under the new supervisor may have been related to her sexual orientation:

> I was closeted at the time, but I have always assumed that it was because I was gay, but when my boss died, in the role of labor relations as you may or may not know, you are often on a funky schedule, you could be negotiating late into the night. So being on time to work meant you know as long as you were there for your first meeting it was fine. The director who took over always hated that, and after three months she issued me a warning letter for lateness, had never spoken to me, had never given me the opportunity to talk about it. I didn't even know that she was watching my time. I went from being sort of the ... superstar person you were going to train to someone who was getting a letter of warning within three months by a new supervisor without any conversation. My assumption has always been, although I never had the conversation, was that she had a problem with me either with the relationship I had with [my former supervisor] Anne who was mentoring me, or because I was gay.

Layoff and dismissal processes can differentially target minority at higher levels of the organization, in what has been termed the minority vulnerability thesis, when employers use meritocratic ideologies to justify layoff decisions that reinforce racial exclusion (Wilson and McBrier, 2005). Specifically, data from a sample of 1,068 white and 676 African American upper-tier employees drawn from a five-year sample demonstrate that the layoffs for African Americans (31 percent) were twice that of whites (16 percent), with higher percentages in the private, non-service industry sectors (Wilson and McBrier, 2005). The results reveal that African Americans are susceptible to layoffs on a broad basis, unstructured by traditional causal factors such as human capital credentials, socioeconomic status, and labor market characteristics (Wilson and McBrier, 2005). The researchers suggest that at privileged levels of the occupational hierarchy, the placement of African Americans in racially delineated positions and constraints on their opportunities to demonstrate competencies for favorable performance evaluations result in race-specific determinants for layoff (Wilson and McBrier, 2005).

In support of the minority vulnerability thesis for layoff, Andrew, a white male human resources administrator in a Southern university, explains how he believes the race and foreign accent of an Asian American administrator led to the effort to target her during the layoff process and deny her bumping privileges:

I am aware of a situation right now of an Asian who doesn't speak English all that well ... She was in a permanent position, but they're talking about cutting her position and technically under our rules she should be allowed to bump someone that has a similar job within that work unit and they don't want to do that.... So it sounds to me like they are after her, because of her race.... One of the people that she would replace is someone is on a limited term, and this Asian person is not on a limited term, so they're arguing that there are different funding sources and she should be not allowed to go into the limited term job.

Diverse administrators may be reluctant to file complaints of discrimination, grievances, or take legal action, due to the difficulty of proving their case, the potential for retaliation, and fear of jeopardizing their employment record. Jon, a white male academic administrator, describes his experiences over a number of years, when minorities, women, and LGBT employees have requested that direct action not be taken that might damage the relationship with their department head:

When you are the only say black or the only woman or the only gay in a department or you are only one of two or three who are in those categories and you report it, there's no way to go back to the department without identifying the individual. So that's part of the problem with the campus-climate surveys that we do. If you go to a department where twenty people are white, and one is black, and you say, 'What's the climate like for racial minorities in this department?' you are likely going to get a heavy majority saying it's great. And the one or two or three will include the minority faculty member. But basically it's fear of some kind of, not again, direct or blatant retaliation, making the situation worse, making the chill colder, making the person feel even more excluded, because now the word is out that she, you know, went to the upper administration. And she's not the first person who has done that, that has happened several times over the years ... people coming in and saying there's a problem, I want you to be aware of it, but I don't want you to take any direct action. I just need basically to talk about it and maybe some advice about how to cope with it....

Survival stress and the fear of unemployment is a constant factor, as shared by a black employee who is the only minority in his department: "So there's that constant awareness on my part, they can snatch what little you have, so that's a constant fear, you know, especially when you have a family to support. So I'm always aware of what can happen" (Tatum, 1997, p. 86).

As a result, the vast resources and unanimity of perspective of the "total institution" overshadow the ability of the isolated minority, female, and/or LGBT administrators to challenge acts of disparate treatment or social closure. The veil of meritocracy and subtlety of process-based discrimination may elude institutional notice and intervention. Double standards as an exclusionary practice contribute to the maintenance of the status quo in performance evaluations, salary reviews, and hiring/termination decisions (Foschi, 2000). The narrative interviews shared in both this and the preceding chapter offer insight into the power of the "total institution" when processes of social closure such as discipline, layoff, and termination differentially target diverse administrators without intervention from the highest levels of the university.

Gauging the Influence of Networks

Informal social networks play a crucial and determinative role in solidifying and advancing power relationships for high-level administrators by providing inside information, resources, contacts, and opportunities for decision making. Networks also affect initial hiring opportunities, as shown by a study of 35,229 applicants to a high technology firm between 1985 and 1994, in which minority applicants lacked access in the precontact stage to the social networks leading to success in being hired (Petersen, Saporta, and Seidel, 2000). This study found that the dividing line in networks was not men against women, but rather whites versus ethnic minorities (Petersen, Saporta, and Seidel, 2000).

The playing field is not level with respect to networks, since networks are embedded within the demographics of organizational context. Diverse individuals face unique constraints that cause their networks to differ in composition and characteristics from those of white males (Ibarra, 1993). A network's instrumentality is a function of both its range in terms of its extent beyond normal work-flow interactions and status in terms of the types of positions in the relevant status hierarchy (see Ibarra, 1995, for review). A study of sixty-three middle managers in four Fortune 500 companies revealed that minority and white middle managers in comparable jobs differed in both the homophily (the degree to which individuals are similar in identity) and intimacy of their networks (Ibarra, 1995). These results suggest the impact of limited availability of same-race others for informal contact as well as the resulting isolation due to lack of close social contacts (Ibarra, 1995). Another study of 418 male and female business-school graduates found that increasing internal visibility through networking was significantly related to the number of promotions and total compensation for men and not for women (Forret and Dougherty, 2004). These results could reflect less access of women to inner, influential organizational circles, individuals, and power coalitions (Forret and Dougherty, 2004).

Within higher echelons of the organization, different interaction contexts exist for majorities and minorities, amplifying stereotypic exchanges between "dominants" and "tokens" in which dominant group members solidify and exaggerate boundary-heightening differences to reinforce common bonds (Ibarra, 1993). Since perceptions of power are based on group stereotypes, minority group members are less likely to be perceived as having power, and as a result, less likely to obtain the power needed to change the dominant view of power (see Ragins, 1997, for review). As a result, even when minorities attain equivalent resources for power, their power can be underestimated and distorted due to stereotypes (Ragins, 1997).

We return to Therese's narrative to illustrate these points within the higher-education workplace. Therese, an African American administrator, explains how an elite group of white women go to lunch on a regular basis and make decisions that have affected her job authority:

> We tend to have a group of people who go to lunch on a regular basis. Instead of holding a meeting for all of the stakeholders, a group of three or four people will go to lunch and make the decisions.... I have a responsibility to pull together some projects and programs and there was a time where I had the authority to make decisions about my programs. And as of lately, after being excluded from these luncheons, I have been directed by my superior to check in with my colleagues to get essentially their permission to move forward with my program, when I didn't have to in the past. But it's not the reverse. Some things in my areas might be impacted greatly....

Therese's description of her exclusion from a prevailing status hierarchy demonstrates the power of informal networking that restricts her job authority and access to inside information and decision making.

Furthermore, as shown in a study of 100 elite white men, high-ranking white men often exist within a "white bubble" that is socially and emotionally isolated from minorities (Feagin and O'Brien, 2003). Elite whites may keep networks segregated on purpose, while sympathetic whites in high positions are still subject to the power and influence of their reference groups and their actions on racial matters (Feagin and O'Brien, 2003). Segregated networks within institutions are at the heart of oppression, since through a cloning process, access to high-ranking contacts and visible assignments is provided to majority group members. Such access can make a difference in critical formal and informal evaluation processes and in the prevention of acts of social closure for diverse administrators.

Internalized Stigma and Collusion with Oppression

As a final consideration in this chapter, we examine how internalized stigma can reverberate not only within an individual's consciousness, but also affect the climate and context of the university workplace. The process of internalizing stigma involves the conscious or unconscious assimilation and acceptance of stigma into an individual's value system and outlook. In colluding with oppression, individuals accept external stigmatizing viewpoints, further perpetuating oppressive perspectives that reflect the devaluation of their own group.

As a result, minorities, women, and LGBT individuals are faced on a daily basis with a struggle against the dominant white racial frame and the patriarchal, gendered, and heterosexual frame, even when they partially collude and acquiesce to this framework. The force of conformity is very powerful within the administrative hierarchy, but may be paralleled by subtle forms of resistance whenever possible.

A complex psychological battle between forms of resistance and compliance for survival can take place with the minds of those subjected to covert and overt discrimination. Awareness of the potential for disparate treatment heightens the stakes in the day-to-day psychological battle waged by diverse administrators. In fact, centuries of racial oppression have made a majority of black Americans into "everyday intellectuals," who have been forced by harsh circumstances to formulate an institutional-racism frame of American society and its institutional practices (Feagin, 2010). What starts as a one-way action by a white discriminator can, to the surprise of the initiator, become an interaction, as diverse individuals either tacitly or overtly contest acts of discrimination (Feagin and Sikes, 1994).

Not only do those stigmatized have the potential for collusion with stigma, but other diverse colleagues can fit the categorization of protagonists, bystanders, assistants, and dissenters when colluding in, observing, or resisting acts of oppression (Picca and Feagin, 2010). Based on the findings of Picca and Feagin's study of 626 college students, the low percentage of college students who took strong or dissenting action in such cases is indicative of the low likelihood of colleagues to intervene and/or provide support to administrators who have been subject to perceived discrimination. Often the risks are simply too high for others to become involved.

Surprisingly, sometimes even those in charge of institutional offices responsible for equal opportunity, affirmative action, or human resources may view issues of race and gender as mostly resolved, and not requiring rigorous attention or vigilance. Take Marilyn, a white female equity and affirmative action official who has served for many years in a large, diverse urban university, who describes the changes the cases that come to her office as follows:

> I have been interested in the changes over time. More of the issues that come to this office are issues of age and disability, but we still have complaints on other grounds as well. And I am also thinking I am seeing instances in younger women and younger minorities, while they may be taken aback by conflict here, are not burdened by that degree of similar conflict. I don't doubt that there are younger professionals, women and minorities, who may experience conflict here, and think, oh my goodness, this could be gender discrimination or race discrimination. But they don't seem to be carrying a long history of grievances on the basis of gender or race, the way my peers, for example, have. For example, I think my first boss at the university who was an African American male, I think he had experienced it all of his life racial discrimination in some form or other, and I don't think that he could envision a time when there would be a workplace even here free of racial discrimination, different treatment based on race. I don't think the younger professional has that history.

By contrast, as Christine, a white female lesbian administrator cited earlier, observes, when she attained the position as Vice President for Human Resources at a prestigious university, her significant institutional stature gives her the latitude and ability to intervene and check discriminatory practices. She notes, however, that the lack of acknowledgement of subtle discrimination by human resource practitioners hinders efforts to correct such practices. As she observes, "… sometimes our [human resource] people are not a pretty people, and they don't acknowledge this or work on it. And it's very frustrating to have HR people who say, 'Oh that's not the reason. . . . ' If anyone, HR people should be the ones who are helping to name it and deal with it."

Returning to Jon's narrative, he similarly identifies the tendency of majority group members on his predominantly white campus to deny the existence of discriminatory incidents as isolated events as well as the implication by white males that women and minorities are being over sensitive. As he perceptively explains:

> . . . they have it in their head . . . that racism, homophobia, and gender discrimination don't really exist here. And so, there's always like an explanation as to why so-and-so said this. . . . 'Oh well, you know him, or I can't believe that anyone in the department thinks that way, oh that's just an isolated incident. . . . ' These isolated incidents keep happening over and over again, basically in the isolated category. I know from my conversations with some of my minority and women colleagues, that that tends to get to them, more than the actual, you know, outright, offensive comment or behavior . . . which they are equipped to deal with.
>
> Because it hasn't happened to them, you know, if you are a white male on this campus and you've been here for twenty-five years, gee, everybody's been really friendly to you, you have never been excluded; they can't imagine it happening to anybody else . . . those very subtle eye contact, tone of voice, body language, differential treatment, those things are not blatantly offensive, not, you know, the kinds of things that you could report or cite as evidence, but just the kind of climate issues. They either will say, 'Oh, that's very isolated . . . ' . . . or they will then suggest that maybe that black person or that woman is overly sensitive, is seeing things that aren't there. . . .

As a result, when university administrators in key institutional roles act as neutral bystanders and either overlook or deny the existence of discrimination as isolated or imagined events, this collusion furthers the purposes of powerful decision makers and can entrench patterns of discrimination in institutional practices, behaviors, and outcomes.

Concluding Perspectives

The accounts of diverse administrators shared in this chapter reveal how formal and even seemingly neutral organizational processes can undermine dignity at work, jeopardize career progress, and serve as a vehicle for particularistic treatment. Why does this matter to the university, to the public, to faculty, staff, and students? Unfairness and discrimination undermine dignity—or the ability to establish a sense of self-respect and self-worth and to enjoy mutual respect (Hodson, 2001). And oppression systematically enforces discrimination through political power than seeks to maintain the status quo and legitimize inequality in domination (McDonald and Coleman, 1999). Violations of dignity can take place through managerial abuse or mismanagement, while acts of resistance and self-realization through productive accomplishments help individuals take back their dignity (Hodson, 2001).

The interview narratives identify significant commonalities in how exclusionary processes unfold across institutional settings, regardless of institutional prestige or reputation, geographic location, or public/private status. Key elements include: 1) continued patterns of white male domination in the executive tier; 2) prevalence of the similarity-attraction paradigm in supervisory-subordinate demography, resulting in potentially disparate employment outcomes; 3) unequal application of organizational processes and the use of double standards; 4) influence of informal opinions and stereotypes upon formal procedures; 5) use of meritocratic explanation to rationalize acts of social closure; 6) exclusion of diverse administrators from visible, decision-making roles and processes; 7) impact of supervisory changes on employment outcomes; 8) lack of due process or recourse for diverse administrators; 9) absence of intervention by executive leadership; and 10) the collusion of bystanders or assistants in acts of exclusion, including other diverse administrators and officials responsible for equity. As can be seen from the narratives in this and the preceding chapter, long-standing records of accomplishment and contributions to the university may be simply overlooked or ignored, while competence and soft skills are questioned.

Much work remains to be done in overcoming barriers to leadership diversity in predominantly white institutions. Strong checks and balances need to be developed to protect diverse administrators from forms of subtle discrimination in the workplace and to ensure that dignity and respect permeate formal processes, practices, and day-to-day interactions. Sustained progress in diversifying Cabinet-level positions is essential, particularly in the roles of Provost, Chief Information Technology Officer, and Chief Financial Officer. Furthermore, recognition and empowerment of the role of the Chief Human Resource Officer position will help address the impact of ascriptive inequality in organizational processes.

The examples cited in this chapter highlight the value of a broadened structure of decision making that allows meaningful discussion and incorporation of diverse perspectives. In particular, the way institutional policies are operationalized will require intensive review in terms of the potential for disparate treatment and disparate impact. Clearly, vulnerability to bias and stereotypes within an institution's personnel systems only promotes devaluation of diverse others and maintenance of privilege in the workplace (Bielby, 2000). Yet the process of discrimination can be disarming and hidden from the neutral observer, since alternative explanations are often possible. Incorporation of due-process rights will help ensure that an objective evaluation of facts occurs and that more than a single institutional decision maker is involved.

In examining whether organizational processes sustain or alter social patterns of disparate treatment and expand, specific areas for consideration include the following:

- What measurements address progress in altering disparate treatment, particularly for those in high-level positions?
- Are consistency and equity attained in the application of policies and processes across organizational divisions?
- Is there institutional scrutiny of how processes such as promotion, compensation, evaluation, and termination may reflect patterns of subtle discrimination?
- Is systematic attention paid to supervisory-subordinate demography and how this relationship impacts career outcomes?
- What mechanisms need to be established to monitor and transform organizational demography?
- Are administrators held accountable when issues of disparate treatment arise?
- Does leadership training include subtle discrimination and social justice issues?

We have seen in this chapter how the collision of power occurs in day-to-day interactions for diverse administrators through the medium of organizational processes. Due to the lack of employment protections, diverse administrators have few options available and can face extraordinary challenges with few alternatives and high professional and personal costs. As universities seek to build an inclusive workplace, systematic review of the potential for differential outcomes on diverse administrators and the impact of subtle discrimination on university processes will enhance psychological safety in the workplace and foster greater organizational justice.

In the next chapter, our focus shifts to the construction of a reconceptualized administrative leadership model that will replace coercive, hierarchical models with a values-driven approach based upon inclusiveness, collaboration, empowerment, and social responsibility (Kezar and Carducci, 2009). Such a model will resonate with the larger, democratic educational purposes of the university. Our analysis will include essential structural elements, and provide best practice examples from research universities that exemplify this new model.

Works Cited

ACE releases first national census of chief academic officers. (2010). Retrieved October 10, 2010, from http://www.acenet.edu/AM/Template.cfm?Section=Home&TEMPLATE=/CM/ContentDisplay.cfm&CONTENTID=31094.

Avey, J. B., West, B. J., and Crossley, C. D. (2008). The association between ethnic congruence in the supervisor-subordinate dyad and subordinate organizational position and salary. *Journal of Occupational and Organizational Psychology*, 81(3), 551–566.

Baldi, S., and McBrier, D. B. (1997). Do the determinants of promotion differ for blacks and whites?: Evidence from the U.S. labor market. *Work and Occupations*, 24(4), 478–497.

Balser, D. B. (2002). Agency in organizational inequality: Organizational behavior and individual perceptions of discrimination. *Work and Occupations*, 29(2), 137–165.

Bielby, W. T. (2000). Minimizing workplace gender and racial bias. *Contemporary Sociology*, 29(1), 120–129.

Brown, W. A. (2008). *Portrait of information technology leaders in higher education: 2008 study of the higher education chief information officer roles and effectiveness.* Retrieved September 29, 2010, from http://www.league.org/publication/whitepapers/files/0708.pdf.

Brown, W. (2009). *A study of CIO roles and effectiveness in higher education.* Retrieved September 29, 2010, from http://campustechnology.com/articles/2009/05/13/a-study-of-cio-roles-and-effectiveness-in-higher-education.aspx.

College and University Professional Association for Human Resources. (2010). *Administrative compensation survey: For the 2009–10 academic year.* Retrieved September 1, 2010, from http://www.cupahr.org/surveys/files/salary0910/AdComp10Executive Summary.pdf.

Collins, S. M. (1997). *Black corporate executives: The making and breaking of a black middle class.* Philadelphia, PA: Temple University Press.

Dovidio, J. F., and Gaertner, S. L. (1996). Affirmative action, unintentional racial biases, and intergroup relations. *Journal of Social Issues*, 52(4), 51–75.

Dovidio, J. F., and Gaertner, S. L. (2000). Aversive racism and selection decisions: 1989 and 1999. *Psychological Science*, 11(4), 315–319.

Dovidio, J. F., Gaertner, S. L., Kawakami, K., and Hodson, G. (2002). Why can't we just get along?: Interpersonal biases and interracial distrust. *Cultural Diversity and Ethnic Minority Psychology,* 8(2), 88–102.

Drentea, P. (1998). Consequences of women's formal and informal job search methods for employment in female-dominated jobs. *Gender and Society,* 12(3), 321–338.

Ekman, R. (2010). The imminent crisis in college leadership. *Chronicle of Higher Education,* 57(5), A88.

Elliott, J. R., and Smith, R. A. (2001). Ethnic matching of supervisors to subordinate work groups: Findings on "bottom-up" ascription and social closure. *Social Problems,* 48(2), 258–276.

Elliott, J. R., and Smith, R. A. (2004). Race, gender, and workplace power. *American Sociological Review,* 69(3), 365–386.

Feagin, J. R. (2006). *Systemic racism: A theory of oppression.* New York: Routledge.

Feagin, J. R. (2010). *The white racial frame: Centuries of racial framing and counter-framing.* New York: Routledge.

Feagin, J. R., and O'Brien, E. (2003). *White men on race: Power, privilege, and the shaping of cultural consciousness.* Boston: Beacon Press.

Feagin, J. R., and Sikes, M. P. (1994). *Living with racism: The black middle-class experience.* Boston: Beacon Press.

Fligstein, N. (1987). The intraorganizational power struggle: Rise of finance personnel to top leadership in large corporations, 1919–1979. *American Sociological Review,* 52(1), 44–58.

Flowers, L. A. (2003). Investigating the representation of African American student affairs administrators: A preliminary study. *National Association of Student Affairs Professionals Journal,* 6(1), 35–43.

Forman, T. A. (2003). The social psychological costs of racial segmentation in the workplace: A study of African Americans' well–being. *Journal of Health and Social Behavior,* 44(3), 332–352.

Forret, M. L., and Dougherty, T. W. (2004). Networking behaviors and career outcomes: Differences for men and women? *Journal of Organizational Behavior,* 25(3), 419–437.

Foschi, M. (2000). Double standards for competence: Theory and research. *Annual Review of Sociology,* 26, 21–42.

Frankl, V. E. (1992). *Man's search for meaning.* Boston: Beacon Press.

Giscombe, K., and Mattis, M. C. (2002). Leveling the playing field for women of color in corporate management: Is the business case enough? *Journal of Business Ethics,* 37(1), 103–119.

Goffman, E. (1961). *Asylums: Essays on the social situation of mental patients and other inmates.* Garden City, NY: Anchor Books.

Green, T. K. (2005). Work culture and discrimination. *California Law Review,* 93(3), 623–684.

Greenhaus, J. H., Parasuraman, S., and Wormley, W. M. (1990). Effects of race on organizational experiences, job performance evaluations, and career outcomes. *The Academy of Management Journal,* 33(1), 64–86.

Hodson, R. (2001). *Dignity at work.* New York: Cambridge University Press.

Ibarra, H. (1993). Personal networks of women and minorities in management: A conceptual framework. *The Academy of Management Review,* 18(1), 56–87.

Ibarra, H. (1995). Race, opportunity, and diversity of social circles in managerial networks. *Academy of Management Journal,* 38(3), 673–704.

Jackson, J. F. L. (2003). Engaging, retaining, and advancing African Americans in student affairs administration: An analysis of employment status. *National Association of Student Affairs Professionals Journal,* 6(1), 9–24.

Jackson, J. F. L., and O'Callaghan, E. M. (2009). *Ethnic and racial administrative diversity: Understanding work life realities and experiences in higher education* (ASHE-ERIC Higher Education Reports, Vol. 35, No. 3). San Francisco: Jossey-Bass.

James, E. H. (2000). Race-related differences in promotions and support: Underlying effects of human and social capital. *Organization Science,* 11(5), 493–508.

Johnsrud, L. K., and Heck, R. H. (1994). Administrative promotion within a university: The cumulative impact of gender. *The Journal of Higher Education,* 65(1), 23–44.

Kanter, R. M. (1977). *Men and women of the corporation.* New York: Basic Books.

Kawakami, K., Dunn, E., Karmali, F., and Dovidio, J. F. (2009, January 9). Mispredicting affective and behavioral responses to racism. *Science,* 323(5911), 276–278.

Kezar, A., and Carducci, R. (2009). Revolutionizing leadership development: Lessons from research and theory. In A. Kezar (Ed.), *Rethinking leadership in a complex, multicultural, and global environment: New concepts and models for higher education* (pp. 1–38). Sterling, VA: Stylus.

Kim, P. S., and Lewis, G. B. (1994). Asian Americans in the public service: Success, diversity, and discrimination. *Public Administration Review,* 54(3), 285–290.

King, J., and Gomez, G. G. (2008). *On the pathway to the presidency: Characteristics of higher education's senior leadership.* Washington, DC: American Council on Education.

Kramer, L. A., and Lambert, S. (2001). Sex-linked bias in chances of being promoted to supervisor. *Sociological Perspectives,* 44(1), 111–127.

Landau, J. (1995). The relationship of race and gender to managers' ratings of promotion potential. *Journal of Organizational Behavior,* 16(4), 391–400.

Lefkowitz, J., and Battista, M. (1995). Potential sources of criterion bias in supervisor ratings used for test validation. *Journal of Business and Psychology,* 9(4), 389–414.

Lyness, K. S., and Heilman, M. E. (2006). When fit is fundamental: Performance evaluations and promotions of upper-level female and male managers. *Journal of Applied Psychology,* 91(4), 777–785.

Mann, T. (2010). Attrition among chief academic officers threatens strategic plans. *Chronicle of Higher Education,* 56(39), A80.

McDonald, P., and Coleman, M. (1999). Deconstructing hierarchies of oppression and adopting a "multiple model" approach to anti-oppressive practice. *Social Work Education,* 18(1), 19–33.

Moss, P., and Tilly, C. (1996). "Soft" skills and race: An investigation of black men's employment problems. *Work and Occupations,* 23(3), 252–276.

National Association of University Business Officers. (2010). *2010 Profile of Higher Education Chief Business and Financial Officers.* Washington, DC: Author.

Petersen, T., and Saporta, I. (2004). The opportunity structure for discrimination. *American Journal of Sociology,* 109(4), 852–901.

Petersen, T., Saporta, I., and Seidel, M. L. (2000). Offering a job: Meritocracy and social networks. *The American Journal of Sociology,* 106(3), 763–816.

Ragins, B. R. (1997). Diversified mentoring relationships in organizations: A power perspective. *The Academy of Management Review,* 22(2), 482–521.

Reskin, B. F. (2000). The proximate causes of employment discrimination. *Contemporary Sociology,* 29(2), 319–328.

Reskin, B. F. (2003). Including mechanisms in our models of ascriptive inequality: 2002 presidential address. *American Sociological Review,* 68, 1–21.

Roscigno, V. J. (2007). *The face of discrimination: How race and gender impact work and home lives.* Lanham, MD: Rowman & Littlefield.

Rowe, M. (2008). *Micro-affirmations & micro-inequities.* Retrieved March 15, 2010, from http://web.mit.edu/ombud/publications/micro-affirm-ineq.pdf.

Sackett, P. R., and DuBois, C. L. Z. (1991). Rater-ratee race effects on performance evaluation. *Journal of Applied Psychology,* 76(6), 873–877.

Sackett, P. R., DuBois, C. L. Z., and Noe, A. W. (1991). Tokenism in performance evaluation. *Journal of Applied Psychology,* 76(2), 263–267.

Saucier, D. A., and Miller, C. T. (2003). The persuasiveness of racial arguments as a subtle measure of racism. *Personality and Social Psychology Bulletin,* 29(10), 1303–1315.

Schieman, S., and McMullen, T. (2008). Relational demography in the workplace and health: An analysis of gender and the subordinate-superordinate role-set. *Journal of Health and Social Behavior,* 49(3), 286–300.

Seidel, M. L., Polzer, J. T., and Stewart, K. J. (2000). Friends in high places: The effects of social networks on discrimination in salary negotiations. *Administrative Science Quarterly,* 45(1), 1–24.

Smith, R. A. (1997). Race, income, and authority at work: A cross-temporal analysis of black and white men (1972–1994). *Social Problems,* 44(1), 19–37.

Smith, R. A. (2002). Race, gender, and authority in the workplace: Theory and research. *Annual Review of Sociology,* 28, 509–542.

Smith, R. A. (2005). Do the determinants of promotion differ for white men versus women and minorities? An exploration of intersectionalism through sponsored and contest mobility processes. *American Behavioral Scientist,* 48(9), 1157–1181.

Smith, R. A., and Elliott, J. R. (2002). Does ethnic concentration influence employees' access to authority? An examination of contemporary urban labor markets. *Social Forces,* 81(1), 255–279.

Tatum, B. D. (1997). *"Why are all the black kids sitting together in the cafeteria?": A psychologist explains the development of racial identity.* New York: Basic Books.

Thomas, D. A., and Gabarro, J. J. (1999). *Breaking through: The making of minority executives in corporate America.* Boston: Harvard Business School Press.

Tsui, A. S., and O'Reilly, C. A., III. (1989). Beyond simple demographic effects: The importance of relational demography in superior-subordinate dyads. *The Academy of Management Journal,* 32(2), 402–423.

Ulrich, D. (1997). *Human resource champions: The next agenda for adding value and delivering results.* Boston: Harvard Business School Press.

Ulrich, D., Allen, J., Brockbank, W., Younger, J., and Nyman, M. (2009). *HR Transformation: Building human resources from the outside in.* New York: McGraw–Hill.

Ulrich, D., and Smallwood, N. (2003). *Why the bottom line isn't!: How to build value through people and organization.* San Francisco: John Wiley & Sons.

Vallas, S. P. (2003). The adventures of managerial hegemony: Teamwork, ideology, and worker resistance. *Social Problems,* 50(2), 204–225.

Wesolowski, M. A., and Mossholder, K. W. (1997). Relational demography in supervisor-subordinate dyads: Impact on subordinate job satisfaction, burnout, and perceived procedural justice. *Journal of Organizational Behavior,* 18(4), 351–362.

Wilson, G., and McBrier, D. B. (2005). Race and loss of privilege: African American/white differences in the determinants of job layoffs from upper-tier occupations. *Sociological Forum,* 20(2), 301–321.

Young, J. R. (2010). *College 2.0: The incredible shrinking CIO: College-tech leaders fear that exclusion from strategic planning will raise costs and hurt institutions.* Retrieved September 27, 2010, from http://chronicle.com/article/College=20The-Incxredible/65442/

4

INDENTURED SERVANTS AND ACADEMIC FREEDOM

Liberation Strategies

> Today, higher education faces a simple choice: reinvention or extinction.... How do we manage, let alone revolutionize these vast and sprawling institutions? How do we make them intellectually agile, responsive to the needs of students, and free from Kafkaesque bureaucracies?
> —*E. Gordon Gee (2009), President,*
> *Ohio State University*

If reinvention is not optional for the survival of the university's educational mission, then what practical steps can the university take to transform administrative culture to be more inclusive? In this chapter we explore the profile and meaning of reconceptualized leadership, discuss approaches that will help the university revolutionize administrative working conditions, share the characteristics of perilous work environments, and identify best practices that will free the university from "Kafkaesque bureaucracies."

Why now? An overarching theme of this book is that diversity is a defining organizational capability that enables the research university to drive the advancement of knowledge in a global economy. Talent is at the forefront of this global imperative—irrespective of race, ethnicity, sexual orientation, gender, disability, age, religious affiliation, and other differentiating characteristics. Furthermore, diversity is an "open systems phenomenon" in that

111

the wider environment, in this case global society, creates demands and pressures to which institutions must respond in order to survive and maintain legitimacy (Siegel, 2003). In a world with permeable boundaries, the relation between higher education and society may be seen as a series of concentric circles, in which colleges and universities are suspended within vast systems and increasingly represent a form of public property (Siegel, 2010). The rise of academic capitalism has meant that groups of actors such as administrators, faculty, academic professionals, and students function within new networks linking higher education to the new economy (Slaughter and Rhoades, 2004). A *glonocal* framework—global, national, and local—reflects the reciprocity of overlapping communities in which outside is becoming "in here" (Marginson, 2004).

Student development is situated within this nested context as students enhance their critical thinking, decision-making capabilities, and cultural fluency in preparation for both civic engagement and cross-boundary relationships in industry, business, and non-profit sectors. Furthermore, universities have increasingly realized the importance of internationalization or the incorporation of intercultural, international, and global dimensions into the delivery of higher education (see Paige, 2005, for review). Diverse learning environments can fuel the psychological challenges and processes of student cognitive and moral reasoning necessary to make a pluralistic democracy succeed (Mayhew and Engberg, 2010). And educated compassion is necessarily part of the affective development that students need to acquire to understand the diverse realities of other individuals (Anderson, 2008). For these reasons, diverse leadership is critical in the integration of cross-cultural, multi-dimensional perspective within the university experience. Diverse administrators serve as important role models for students in a glonocal model built upon reciprocity, mutual understanding, and networked interaction.

The unchecked persistence of forms of subtle discrimination at the core of the university's administrative processes threatens institutional integrity, accountability, and what Gordon Gee calls "the pride of place" that the university needs to occupy at the center of civic life (Gee, 2009). The external public accountability of the university, as an open system, is a check on arbitrary power and the corruption of power that occurs through manipulation and malfeasance (Trow, 1998). Accountability—whether legal, financial, or moral/intellectual—strengthens the legitimacy of institutions, and this legitimacy can be compromised when arbitrary power is exercised through manipulation in secret (Trow, 1998).

Furthermore, as minorities, women, and LGBT individuals are oppressed and marginalized in predominantly white institutions, not only do they suffer personally and in their families and communities, but the institutions will suffer and may eventually decline and deteriorate (Feagin, 2010). A society that ignores the talent, creativity, and understanding of diverse individuals "irresponsibly risks its future" (Feagin, 2010, p. 213).

As we have seen in the preceding chapters, the alarming swiftness, sheer impunity, and unchallenged subjectivity exercised in acts of social closure involving diverse administrators reinforces the dispensability rather than the sustainability of diverse talent and the analogy to indentured servitude. Even during the course of this study, three women and/or minority administrators of the forty participating in the survey we conducted disappeared from the positions they had held. These administrators were either managed out or elected retirement as the only option available. In an ironic twist that we have noted in several previous instances, two of the three administrators served in a chief diversity officer or affirmative action role. As we have noted earlier, a number of minority and/or female interviewees expressed fear and concern about sharing their perspectives in interviews for this book, due to the potential for retaliation and possible retribution.

What then is the realistic likelihood of change in the administrative model? Is the potential for employment conditions that promote greater stability and security a genuine possibility or will the plight of diverse administrators continue to be overlooked as unimportant? In the next section, we discuss why a new leadership model is beneficial to the overall success of the university and why faculty, staff, and administrators need to work collectively in support of administrative change. The optimal alignment of leadership practices, we argue, is now a necessary condition for institutional success in light of rapidly shifting environmental conditions, intense resource competition, and the need to preserve shared governance and democratic values in the American university.

Why a Reconceptualized Leadership Model Is Necessary

A recent study of world-class universities concluded that such institutions possess three main characteristics: 1) a high concentration of talent; 2) abundant resources; and 3) favorable governance structures that enhance strategic vision, flexibility, and innovation and that support decision making and resource management unencumbered by bureaucracy (Salmi, 2009). Educational institutions represent peculiar combinations of academic guilds and bureaucratic functions (Trow, 1998). Reconciliation of the power dynamic involved in the struggle between the business-oriented, command-and-control model of administration with the academic values of autonomy, academic freedom, and shared governance is essential to building organizational capacity. Institutional effectiveness is dependent upon strategic integration and effective deployment of organizational resources, whether or not the institution has the administrative capacity to fulfill its mission and aspirations (Toma, 2010).

The Leadership Environment Today

The environment in higher education has been compared to a "perfect storm" in which wind, sea, and rain combine with cataclysmic force (Tierney, 2004). Five major interests at stake in higher education today are social justice, competence (excellence), academic freedom, autonomy/accountability, and decentralization/centralization (Rhoades, 1983). At the heart of the storm is the fundamental purpose of academic institutions, which is to embody ideas and not to create products (Birnbaum, 2004). Yet external competition, debates over quality, and the changing role of the state in funding higher education create the need for a more cohesive university culture to respond to dynamic, environmental conditions (Tierney, 2004).

The system of shared governance that preserves the rights of faculty to participate in important decision-making processes has come under question with the increasingly market-driven emphasis on efficiency. Yet "hard" (or rational) governance or the structures and systems that define authority relationships must be distinguished from "soft" governance that involves the systems of social connections and interactions that maintain group and individual norms (Birnbaum, 2004). An emerging perspective emphasizes that while structures of governance may impact *efficiency*, institutional *effectiveness* is improved through leadership, relationships, and trust (see Kezar, 2004, for review). Most decisions occur outside the formal system of governance and provide the opportunity for building social capital that, in turn, leads to trust and cooperation (Birnbaum, 2004). Rather than a structural perspective, the key to understanding the landscape of higher education lies in examination of the power, relationships, belief systems, and struggles between groups that have input into the system (Rhoades, 1983).

Twenty-first Century Leadership Principles

Twenty-first century leadership is both inclusive and integrative. It reverses the traditional view of the leader as charismatic soloist, and replaces this concept with shared power, consensus, and collaboration. Prior hierarchically oriented leadership models based upon power, control, and individualism, have been supplanted by context-bound, process-oriented, collective leadership assumptions (Kezar and Carducci, 2009). As a result, integrative leaders understand how to capitalize upon the pluralistic processes of convergence, confluence, and engagement.

Polycentric governance and participatory management reorient hierarchical organizing principles to a horizontal framework in which the social issue or problem that is normally the object of intervention by social actors, becomes the subject as social actors become stakeholders in the problem (Siegel, 2009). Collective action, in which different sectors of the organization come to view themselves as mutual stakeholders in social problems, enhances and enlarges the identities of institutional actors (Siegel, 2009). An essential aspect of such collective action is procedural justice that reinforces the legitimacy of organizational decisions and builds trust in leadership through predictability and mutually reinforcing relationships of identity, support, and confidence (Birnbaum, 2004).

Evidence of this shift in focus has been demonstrated in a six-year American Council of Education Project on Leadership and Institutional Transformation undertaken in twenty-three colleges and universities, which discovered that transforming institutions relies upon five core strategies: 1) senior administrative support; 2) visible action; 3) flexible vision; 4) collaborative leadership; and 5) staff development (Eckel and Kezar, 2003). These empirical results emphasize three requirements: senior leadership engagement, willingness to take concrete action, and commitment to collaborative practices (Eckel and Kezar, 2003).

Identity Development and Twenty-first Century Leadership

Identity development is a defining aspect of the contemporary leadership model for women, minority, and LGBT administrators, given existing stereotypes and preconceptions about leadership. Diverse individuals occupy different structural positions in the workplace and encounter conflicting cultural attitudes about their identities in relation to leadership positions (Ely and Rhode,

2010). From an individual perspective, identity is a central focus for a model of leadership skill since it provides a significant structure for the organization of significant knowledge, is a source of motivation and direction in developmental situations, and allows access to personal materials (such as core values and stories) that will help leaders motivate and understand subordinates (Lord and Hall, 2005).

In closing the gap between identity and image, the challenge for diverse leaders remains to bring their provisional and professional identities into greater congruence, particularly since they generally will have fewer supports for conveying a leadership image and receive less latitude for mistakes (Ely and Rhode, 2010). Provisional identities are trials for more fully elaborated professional identities, while professional identity combines both personal and social identities and emerges through social interaction (Ibarra, Snook, and Ramo, 2010). And, as shown by a study of thirty-four professionals in two firms, it is a process of experimentation and adaptation to improve the fit between individual identity and the work environment that tests the repertoire of possibilities (Ibarra, 1999).

Integration of the leadership role with the core self for diverse administrators may involve contradictions such as, for example, the contrast between the traditionally masculine attributes associated with leadership and the feminine identity (Ely and Rhode, 2010). Integration of identities also means addressing the intersectionality of multiple dimensions of difference—such as race, gender, class, ability, and sexual orientation.

Diverse leaders battle with external challenges to their leadership identity in terms of stereotypes, biases, and misperceptions about their leadership style, competence, and abilities. The process of identity development developed by Cross (1971, 1978) explains how individuals isolate, then internalize, and re-integrate a facet or facets of their identity such as race, ethnicity, gender, and sexual orientation into their identity matrix (see Tatum, 1997, for review). This development involves five distinct phases: 1) *pre-encounter* with the dominant culture and its normed expectations of white, male, heterosexual privilege; 2) *encounter* with stereotypes and the personal impact of a devalued position; 3) *immersion* in the multiplicity of one's own identity; 4) *internalization* of a positive leadership identity that embraces the value of their own difference; and 5) *internalized commitment* to ongoing action in support of diverse others (see Tatum, 1997, for review). This developmental process is circular and ongoing, rather than linear and finite, like a spiral staircase, as individuals revisit earlier phases they may have passed through (Tatum, 1997).

The new administrative model requires an expanded organizational focus that includes explicit recognition of the impact of organizational demographics, structural underrepresentation, and prevailing cultural biases/stereotypes upon the success of diverse administrators. As a result, university leadership programs will benefit from attention to the substantive challenges faced by diverse leaders and their professional need for identity integration in the face of prevailing attitudinal barriers.

Furthermore, from a structural perspective, university selection processes need to support the appointment of diverse professionals in line positions with genuine authority and resources to overcome patterns of ghettoization in fields such as affirmative action and diversity. In this regard, Caroline, a white female provost in a prominent research university, notes the barriers minorities face in taking on administrative roles as well as the concentration of minorities in roles such as the diversity officer:

> I do think some are able to get past [the barriers] and have very strong influence. But I think it discourages people who could be very good in administration, but get beaten down before they get to that point. The other thing that I kind of worry about is very often when you see administrators of color it's because they are the head of a diversity office and not the vice chancellor of business and administrative services or the vice chancellor of planning and budget.
>
> There is still discrimination but it's much more subtle than the kind of discrimination that I used to see … but it's still there … when you're looking for people who might be good for positions, it's the same names come up over and over again and they are usually sort of senior white male.

In the next sections, we examine specific policies, systems, and programs that specifically address the perilous working conditions of diverse administrators. These best practice examples will help foster greater leadership continuity, avoid costly litigation, provide greater administrative employment stability, and foster the retention and job satisfaction of diverse administrators.

Exemplary Institutional Practices and Strategies

A number of research universities have launched innovative faculty initiatives that focus upon the need for a culture of inclusion through a process of rigorous self-assessment and action plans. While the focus of such plans has rarely included administrators, the principles and concepts provide an analytical framework that can be more broadly extended to other employee groups. For example, as Susan Hockfield, President of the Massachusetts Institute of Technology, writes in her preface to the ground-breaking, empirically based Initiative for Faculty Race and Diversity, "Creating a culture of inclusion is not an optional exercise; it is the indispensable precondition that enables us to capitalize on our diverse skills, perspectives and experiences, so that we can better advance the fundamental research and education mission ..." (Hockfield, 2010, para. 4).

Institutional policies create the conditions for discourse, interaction, and behavior, in the context of a respectful and hospitable environment. And the language of policy is critical since, following a post-structuralist perspective, power and oppression are embedded in daily practices that are accessed through language (Kezar, 2010). Changing how people make meaning through language involves more than simply changing policies, and requires digging deeper (Kezar, 2010). Yet to be effective, policies need to operationalize how the organization reviews its own internal processes such as hiring, promotion, evaluation, compensation, and disciplinary action through mechanisms that promote equity and accountability.

As an example of digging deeper into the change process through both discourse and accountability, Princeton University's policy on "Respect for Others" specifically links a language of respect to sanctions for abusive or harassing behavior that demeans others because of personal characteristics or beliefs. The policy moves beyond mere statements to actual consequences for violations of community norms:

> Respect for the rights, privileges, and sensibilities of each other is essential in preserving the spirit of community at Princeton. Actions which make the atmosphere intimidating, threatening, or hostile to individuals are therefore regarded as serious offenses. Abusive or harassing behavior, verbal or physical, which demeans, intimidates, threatens, or injures another because of personal characteristics or beliefs or their expression, is subject to University disciplinary sanctions as described above. Examples of personal characteristics or beliefs include but are not limited to sex, sexual orientation, gender identity, race, ethnicity, national origin, religion, and disability. Making tolerance of such behavior or submission to it a condition of employment, evaluation, compensation, or advancement is an especially serious offense.... The University seeks to promote the full inclusion of

all members and groups in every aspect of University life. (The Trustees of Princeton University, 2010, Respect for Others, para. 1)

Mutual respect requires special sensitivity to issues of race and ethnicity. Expressions of racial or ethnic bias directed at individuals or groups undermine the civility and sense of community on which the well-being of the University depends. They devalue the distinctive contributions of the individuals affected and impair their ability to contribute their views and talents to the community and to benefit fully from participating in it. By alienating those individuals, they harm the whole community. The University calls on all its members to display the appropriate sensitivity and to challenge expressions of racial or ethnic bias whenever they encounter them. (The Trustees of Princeton University, 2010, Respect for Others, para. 3)

Another example of a holistic approach that creates a language of respect and dignity is the long-standing "Principles of Community" developed at the University of California at Davis in 1990 through a collaborative process and reaffirmed in 2010 ("Principles of Community Reaffirmed," 2010). The "Principles of Community" are linked to specific university policies and reinforce the basic values of dignity, justice, freedom of expression, respect, and diversity:

We affirm the inherent dignity in all of us, and we strive to maintain a climate of justice marked by respect for each other. We acknowledge that our society carries within it historical and deep-rooted misunderstandings and biases, and therefore we will endeavor to foster mutual understanding among the many parts of our whole.... We promote open expression of our individuality and our diversity within the bounds of courtesy, sensitivity and respect. ("The Principles of Community," n.d., para. 2)

We confront and reject all manifestations of discrimination, including those based on race, ethnicity, gender, age, disability, sexual orientation, religious or political beliefs, status within or outside the university, or any of the other differences among people which have been excuses for misunderstanding, dissension or hatred. We recognize and cherish the richness contributed to our lives by our diversity. We take pride in our various achievements, and we celebrate our differences. ("The Principles of Community," n.d., para. 4)

The "Make 100 Commitments to Promote Diversity and Inclusion" Program at Kent State University represents an additional example of a university-wide initiative designed to promote acceptance, understanding, and mutual respect with a particular focus on promoting Inclusive Excellence at the departmental level ("100 Commitments," 2010).

Foundational policies that affirm the values of respect, social justice, diversity, and inclusion, prepare the groundwork for process-based policies that strengthen employment protections for administrators. In the next section, we provide examples of how institutional processes can provide the essential checks and balances needed to increase organizational scrutiny, eliminate forms of differential treatment, and promote greater inclusion of diverse administrators.

Building an Architecture of Inclusion: Design of Formal Processes

The formal architecture of a more stable and internally consistent administrative structure requires policies and processes that enhance organizational and procedural justice. Specific areas for policy development that address more secure and equitable working conditions for administrators include multi-year contracts, due process rights, grievance procedures, and review of evaluation and compensation determinations.

From an overall perspective, Pennsylvania State University's "Framework to Foster Diversity at Penn State: 2010–2015," a comprehensive third-generation, five-year diversity plan, makes the accountability link from principles to action in one of its seven key challenges "Diversifying University Leadership and Management" ("A Framework to Foster Diversity," n.d.). This challenge emphasizes the need for leaders who possess the experience, ability, and drive to foster diversity throughout the organization, enhance articulation between executive leadership and departments, and promote diverse leadership teams in administrative, strategic planning, and governing bodies ("A Framework to Foster Diversity," n.d.). The focus of the plan overall is to strengthen university-wide performance indicators and to move from "measuring activity to measuring achievement" ("A Framework to Foster Diversity," n.d., p. 6).

Similarly, the Texas A&M University Diversity Plan establishes structures, processes, and policies that hold units accountable and actually rewards units and individuals for demonstrated progress in creation of an environment that treats the diversity of individual identities and ideas equitably ("Texas

A&M University Diversity Plan," n.d.). Progress in representation and climate can result in increases to a unit's base funding calculated based on the size of the merit pool for the year (usually approximately 10 percent) ("Texas A&M University Diversity Plan," n.d.).

Both of these plans provide examples of a comprehensive approach to diversity and inclusion based upon concrete performance indicators, data, and outcomes. Without the link to measurable outcomes, diversity plans will remain no more than window dressing or rhetorical statements without the ability to transform organizational culture.

Multi-year Contracts

The concept of a multi-year contract for administrators represents a key strategy that will help stabilize administrative employment and narrow the gap between administrators and other university employees such as faculty and unionized staff. Multi-year contracts within the research university are frequently awarded to head coaches and presidents, but rarely applied to other non-academic administrative positions. The opportunity for multi-year contracts would represent substantive improvement in employment security and enhance performance by removing the constant concern about renewal when contracts are offered for only one-year terms.

Multi-year contracts can be structured as rolling contracts with evaluation at the end of each year and longer notice periods for non-renewal dependent upon longevity. These contracts may parallel those offered to non-faculty research appointments at a number of leading research universities that range from three to five years and offer a measure of stability that improves the quality of programs and fosters greater individual productivity ("Examples of Appointments," n.d.). Such contracts have even been proposed for contingent faculty as a way of stabilizing employment and heightening their participation in governance (Kezar, Lester, and Anderson, 2006).

Due Process and Procedural Rights

As a result of their tenuous status, administrators for the most part have few due process rights, other than in situations of blatant discrimination and appeal through non-discrimination policies. Yet as documented in research findings and the interview narratives, the opportunity structure for subtle discrimination provided by at will status has resulted in heightened vulnerability and differential treatment for diverse administrators in university processes. By contrast, a collective and concerted policy approach that emphasizes organizational justice for all employment groups would no longer relegate administrators to separate-but-unequal status relative to their faculty and classified staff counterparts.

A decisive step in this direction, but one unlikely to be implemented at many institutions, is to offer grievance processes for administrators and consider incorporation of grievance or complaint committees of peers in the review process. Although even the suggestion of peer review is absent from most policies pertaining to administrators, improvements in this area would provide greater procedural justice by incorporating a review of decisions by a third party. At best, administrators generally only have access in appeal processes to review by the same chain of command that issues a decision originally.

Southern Oregon University's "Grievance Procedure for Administrators" represents a prominent example of the incorporation of peer review in administrative grievance processes ("Grievance Procedure for Administrators," 2005). The policy includes both informal and formal grievance procedures for personnel actions including compensation, dismissal, and disciplinary employment practices, or denial of procedural rights in relation to non-renewal or appointment ("Grievance Procedure for Administrators," 2005). It establishes the opportunity for formal collegial review through a hearing committee of five administrators appointed by the associate vice president for human resources, with final decision by the president on behalf of both the campus and the Oregon University System ("Grievance Procedure for Administrators," 2005).

Integrated Conflict Management Systems

As documented in the interview narratives, diverse administrators may have few internal organizational resources available to them due to their relatively high position in the institutional hierarchy. Nonetheless, universities will benefit from the development of an integrated range of options for confidential discussion and problem-solving. Formal grievance processes often are not a viable alternative due to lack of sufficient evidence of wrong-doing, complex webs of problems, fear of retaliation, and the difficulty of dealing with the damaging, cumulative effects of subtle discrimination (Rowe, 1993; Rowe, 1996). By contrast, an integrated conflict management system provides multiple access points, a range of options, and gatekeepers that represent diversity of race, gender, and sexual orientation (Rowe, 1996).

An integrated conflict management system optimally includes investment in a robust employee relations network, separate from the labor-relations function in human resources as well as a confidential Employee Assistance program, and mediation or informal dispute resolution services. Additionally, a number of universities have established an Ombuds position and office to serve as a neutral third party, despite the fact that such positions typically report to the President. The Harvard University Medical School, Dental School, and School of Public Health have incorporated the role of the ombudsperson into policy as part of the informal resolution of discrimination and harassment complaints ("Harvard Medical School," 2008). Another rich resource for building an integrated conflict management program can be found on the MIT Ombuds Web site that reflects the pioneering work of Mary Rowe, University Ombudsperson since 1973, and provides an array of publications and self-help tools ("Mission," n.d.).

From a process perspective, an integrated system is not only cost-effective in terms of avoidance of litigation and employer protection, it also provides individuals with small choices and realistic options that will make it more likely that they will come forward in a timely fashion (Rowe, 1993).

Diversity as a Criterion in Management Performance Review

Although diversity and inclusion often have been incorporated in management review processes, the real test is whether diversity is a superfluous evaluative criterion or is integrally linked to measurable accomplishments. In this regard, the University of California Senior Management Group Performance Management Review Process provides an example of linking diversity and accountability through establishment of standards and competencies for diversity as well as principles of community; collaboration and communication; accountability and governance; and inspiring innovation and leading change ("Senior Management Group Performance," 2010). All of these competencies are integral to transformational change in support of diversity. In addition to the annual review process, a five-year Senior Leadership Assessment provides managerial coaching and development rather than evaluation of achievements and includes consultation with a broad range of constituencies to collect input and provide feedback ("Senior Management Group Performance," 2010).

Professional Development, Mentoring, and Institutional Safety Nets

Professional development and mentoring programs that create opportunities for career growth and provide strategies for navigating the internal organization are essential components in a culture of inclusion. Such programs include sabbaticals, affinity groups, and formal/informal mentoring programs. In addition, consideration may be given to creation of a home place or space within the university where diverse individuals can minimize marginality, center experiences, and discuss both professional and personal issues in an atmosphere of psychological safety (Jordan-Zachery, 2004).

Sabbatical Leave

Sabbatical leave programs often do not include administrators, despite the fact that such leaves are important channels for professional growth, completion of degree programs, and research. A prominent example of an administrative sabbatical program is the Board Policy of the Minnesota State Colleges and Universities that establishes up to a one-year sabbatical leave for eligible administrators with six years of service for education, training, or experience related to management responsibilities at either no pay, partial pay, or full pay ("Minnesota State Colleges & Universities," 2009; "Policy 6-314," 1997). The University of Utah offers administrators with three years of service a more specifically focused paid leave of three months to complete the final phase of a doctoral program of value to the university ("4.7 Sabbatical Leaves," 1999).

Support and Affinity Groups

Many research universities have established affinity or networking groups for faculty and staff that serve as a resource for individuals outside of their own departments to gather and share ideas relating to professional development, recruitment/retention, community outreach, and related concerns. One of the pitfalls of such groups, however, may be to replicate the notion of segregation or exclusion when such groups are based only on visible characteristics such as race, ethnic background, and gender (Goins, 2010).

To counteract such trends, groups can be organized around different social identities or interests or around common social justice issues. For example, the Human Resources Department at Syracuse University assists in furthering the formation of a wide range of staff affinity groups that are designed to support diversity and inclusion, strengthen the University community, enhance the workplace, and support professional and personal development ("Exempt & Non-Exempt Staff," n.d.). In addition to groups relating to racial identity, other networking groups include a bereavement group, community service group, family caregivers group, young professionals affinity group, and a working mothers group ("Exempt & Non-Exempt Staff," n.d.).

Coaching and Mentoring Programs

Diversified mentoring programs have received attention in the research literature in terms of the relational demography of homogeneous versus cross-gender and cross-racial relationships as these relationships unfold in a context of restricted power (see Ragins, 1997, for review). Mentoring fulfills multiple functions including career development, psychosocial support, and role modeling (Ragins, 1997). Career development functions of mentoring include coaching, sponsorship, protection, and increased exposure through challenging assignments, whereas psychosocial functions address interpersonal enhancement of the protégés sense of competency and self-efficacy (see Ragins and Cotton, 1999, for review).

Theoretically, such programs have substantial organizational benefits in terms of cultural diversity, preservation of intellectual capital, and improved leadership capacity through reciprocal learning relationships that foster trust, respect, and commitment (see Zellers, Howard, and Barcic, 2008, for review). Yet from a practical perspective, diverse administrators face significant challenges in finding mentors who can provide psychosocial support due to the scarcity of minority and female role models as well as the tendency of white men who hold most positions of authority to seek social comfort with those they work with and promote (Ragins, 1997; Thomas, 1990; Zellers, Howard, and Barcic, 2008).

As confirmed in a study of 1,162 male and female respondents in three professional fields, greater psychosocial and career benefits may be obtained from informal mentoring, given the longer-term nature of such relationships that are based upon mutual identification and perceptions of interpersonal comfort and competence (Ragins and Cotton, 1999). As a result, formal mentoring programs cannot be considered as a substitute for informal mentoring, but can serve as a springboard for the development of informal relationships (Ragins and Cotton, 1999).

The university has been slower to formalize its practices in response to higher education's changing organizational dynamics and demographics (Zellers, Howard, and Barcic, 2008). Most existing mentoring programs focus upon faculty development. And despite the importance of contextually based mentoring, administrative mentoring programs, especially those that provide career development opportunities for women and minorities, tend to be concentrated at the national or regional level (Strathe and Wilson, 2006).

Several prominent programs offer campus-based opportunities for tenured faculty to gain senior administrative experience such as the University of Kansas Senior Administrative Fellows Program ("Senior Administrative Fellows Program," 2010) and the Illinois State Administrative Fellows Program ("Administrative Fellows Program," 2008). A fully featured mentorship program is offered by the Pennsylvania State University to both staff and faculty during a one-year period in which mentors and fellows work together to design the experiences that include trustee meetings, state budget hearings, and meetings with senior administrators including the president and provost ("Administrative Fellows Program," 2010). In a different type of mentoring initiative, the University of Washington offers a professional coaching program through the Office of Human Resources ("Professional Coaching," 2007). A number of institutions offer women's mentoring initiatives such as the "Women Supporting Women Mentor Program" at Carnegie Mellon University ("Women Supporting Women's Mission," n.d.).

Institutional Safety Nets

The concept of institutional safety nets has not been implemented in a systematic fashion, although a significant number of universities has implemented safe zones or ally programs to provide assistance and support to lesbian, gay, bisexual, and transgendered employees in an atmosphere of confidentiality. Safe-zone training focuses upon educational components that allow participants to examine their own internalized homophobia and heterosexism. Safe-zone symbols that include an inverted pink triangle in a green circle and a rainbow flag or rainbow triangle identify persons as supporters of the LGBT community with whom individuals can discuss issues related to sexual identity and gender expression. Extension of the concept of safe zones to include other aspects of diversity such as race, gender, and disability could provide avenues for building alliances and identifying supporters.

Our discussion now turns from specific policies and programs that build an infrastructure of support for diverse administrators to the characteristics of unwelcoming, chilly, or even hostile environments for diverse administrators, and ways that they may align expectations with reality when evaluating job offers or career opportunities.

Warning Signs of a Non-welcoming Environment

Many common themes emerge from both the research literature and the accounts of women, minority, and LGBT administrators in this study that identify perilous work environments in the university. Patterns of subtle discrimination experienced by diverse administrators unfold with remarkable similarity, particularly in situations where demographic differences of race and/or gender exist between supervisor and supervisee. The six underlying themes described here form the tactical weaponry of new and clandestine forms of discrimination that elude notice and can be dismissed as imaginary or based upon meritocratic justification.

Restricted Authority and Resources in Line Supervisory Positions

Diverse administrators with line authority can experience the impact of exclusionary management practices not only upon themselves, but also upon the units or departments they oversee. Restricted resources, limited authority in terms of influential decisions affecting employees they supervise such as in promotions or compensation, lack of access to information, and exclusion from decision-making venues can undermine the effectiveness of diverse administrators and create the perception that they do not manage as efficiently as their white male counterparts. As we have seen from Julie's narrative, the ability to take strong action in disciplinary situations may be extremely limited, fostering an impression of weakness. Units under the supervision of diverse administrators may feel the brunt of such exclusionary practices on a regular basis, diminishing the department's effectiveness and creating the perception that the department is not functioning well.

In a telling example of this phenomenon, Caroline, the white female provost cited earlier, describes her exclusion as the only female dean from key academic dean meetings, based upon both her gender and the lack of professional respect for the area of responsibility she managed at the time. She also notes the prevailing practices of exclusion of women from informal decision-making opportunities and academic discourse, as well as the financial impact of such exclusion on the division she oversaw:

> ... but what it means is that women just do not fit into the discourse and that leaves us at a disadvantage when we have to go into a meeting when there is a lot of discussion around things that have already been talked about in other settings.... the deans convene but they convene by the academic units. And for some reason [my unit] is not [considered] an academic unit which means that I am never in those meetings.... I think it is both gender and a bias against working professionals.... But it actually has had some pretty negative effects on my unit's understanding of budget matters. Because there have been times in the past, before I was dean, the previous dean was also a woman, and because she wasn't in discussions with the other deans she did not know that she could contest fees that were assessed against the units, so this unit ended up paying far more in the fees than the other units ... huge amounts of money. I think that more likely a male dean would have been at least clued into those negotiations, even if he wasn't brought in on the little deans meeting. I think that he would have been clued in that there was room for negotiations on these monies.

Distortion and Stereotypes in Relation to Attributes of Power

We have noted research that links perceived competence to power and describes how stereotypes and attributions of weakness, lack of initiative, and incompetence influence the acquisition and maintenance of power for diverse individuals (see Ragins, 1997; Ragins and Sundstrom, 1989, for example). Stereotypical perceptions limit the efficacy and authority of diverse administrators, requiring continual justification of their work and their professionalism. Such perceptions may persist despite significant records of accomplishments and contributions. In this regard, Sonia, a Hispanic female administrator who reports to the highest levels in her institution, describes the lack of recognition of her expertise by her superiors:

> ... and I don't think it is just related to my race ... but it is also related to my gender, and the size of my body, I'm short.... And I do think people make visual judgments.... I have a pretty responsible position right now.... The challenge that I face is that I am always having to have an

authority whether it is the law or a lawyer or previous risks that haven't gone well as resources for me, rather than their accepting my expertise and essentially recognizing the many years of experience that I have had. So I would say that has been a challenge for me, and I just keep at it.... It's just that ... I feel as though I have to go through more of the justification for my credentials and essentially trying to confirm that I deserve to be at the table.

Invisibility and Repeated Exclusion from Having a Voice

A repeated theme raised by a number of diverse administrators is restricted participation in meetings appropriately related to their job roles or from having a voice in such forums. Supervisors often determine how high-level meetings are structured in terms not only of who is invited to attend but also the level of participation of the individuals in these meetings. Other employees present at these meetings quickly tap into subtle, verbal, and nonverbal scripts and cues that indicate validation or omission of specific individuals. Supervisory exclusion may include understating or omitting accomplishments, giving credit to others for work performed, limiting an individual's ability to contribute meaningfully in public forums, and not providing access to higher-level executives. As an African American administrator, Lisa explains the exclusion from participation faced by diverse administrators in this manner, "The other thing of being outside of the mainstream, where you're not what you used to call part of the old-boy system or what I call the old-boy/girl system is that you are not going to be in the conversation, or at the water fountain."

Collegial interactions may reinforce such patterns of invisibility ranging from forms of subtle unconscious discrimination to active bullying, particularly when unchecked by upper administration. As an example of how courageous intervention "in the moment" can check such behaviors, however, Christine, the white lesbian administrator cited earlier in the book, describes her response when colleagues avoid addressing questions directly to the head of Institutional Diversity who is an African American woman.

> My colleague and I work closely together so I get to see these micro-experiences that she has in meetings with other colleagues. So I find myself saying, 'I see that you directed that question to me and not to Jeannine, why is that? That's not my field, that's Jeannine's field.'
>
> ... there's a million of those micro-experiences where you know they won't look her in the eye. Because I am in a room with her sometimes two

or three hours in a day based on the work that we do, I get to have the opportunity to get to see what it's like to be a black woman ... and to have these things occur, based on people's assumptions and prejudices and ... most of the time, they just don't really, really, really understand their own actions and the impact that they cause.... And when you point it out, first they deny it, and then they try to deal with it, and some of them deal with it well and some of them they don't know what you're talking about.

Later when she and I leave the room she'll say or I will say 'Did you see that?' But when she gets really frustrated with it, she picks up the phone and she's a very religious woman and she says, 'Can I swear?' and we just talk through it and figure out a strategy for how to deal with it. Well you know, I think it's actually a great source of learning for me. Just like people don't know how to experience gay people because they don't know gay people ... I am getting to experience by working closely with her what it can be like to be black and what those micro-experiences do as they add up.... I have to tell people I'm gay for them to discriminate against me. People can be discriminatory against people of color, and not even realize it because it's their own inner stuff.

The examples cited in this book of the exclusion of diverse administrators from decision-making forums illustrate the power of acts of omission as a form of covert discrimination.

The Fear Factor: Bullying and Veiled Threats

The phenomenon of psychical terror or mobbing in workplaces represents the culmination of the forces of subtle discrimination and sustained bullying over a period of time. The pioneering researcher Heinz Leymann defined psychical terror as hostile, unethical communication directed systematically by one or more persons toward one individual. Leymann characterized such systematic bullying as manipulation with five dimensions: 1) manipulation of the victim's reputation (undermining accomplishments, rumor mongering, slandering); 2) communication toward the victim (not allowing the victim to express himself); 3) social circumstances (isolation); 4) the nature of work (assignment of humiliating or meaningless work tasks); and 5) threats (Leymann, 1990). Based upon his inventory of Psychological Terrorization, Leymann concluded that such situations are not linear in the sense that mobbing is more or less intense: either an individual is a victim or he/she is not (Leymann, 1990). Consistent with the definition of mobbing and psychical terror, several interviewees identified key elements of mobbing and manipulation including situations in which employment was threatened by supervisors, communication was cut off, and isolation was intensified. We have noted earlier that women, minority, and LGBT administrators are particularly vulnerable to this type of attack due to unstable employment conditions, high visibility, and social isolation.

For example, Caroline, the white female Provost, described how earlier in her career as a faculty member she had been threatened with not attaining tenure if she did not engage in an unethical practice. Note the introduction of pressure to perform unethical actions that was comingled with the bullying Caroline experienced. Unethical demands were also a factor in Claudia's account of the bullying she experienced. As Caroline relates, "I had somebody who controlled my future and wanted me to do something which I didn't find ethical actually but it was again one of those 'he-said-she-said' situations and he had the power and the ear of everybody and my solution was to leave. I left the institution.... " Caroline indicated that she believed this incident to be a case of gender discrimination, and that her supervisor really wanted a male in her role.

Lack of Coaching and Magnification of Mistakes

The narratives of Mark, Lisa, Claudia, Julie, Michael, and Therese provide examples of how supervisors fail to provide coaching at critical intervals and how any missteps can be magnified and misconstrued. The application of double standards coupled with a lack of supervisory support create treacherous and highly stressful work conditions that make it difficult for diverse leaders to be effective in their roles. Furthermore, when channels for informal supervisory communication are limited or even nonexistent, diverse administrators may not have the opportunity to build rapport, counteract rumors or gossip, and present alternate perspectives that influence workplace outcomes.

Rapid, Irreversible Turning Points

An insightful study of eighty-four new and midcareer faculty that included both women and minorities concluded that turning points in the tenure journey occur with surprising and devastating speed and appear to be irreversible (Boice, 1993). Such turning points are marked by behavioral indicators including heightened self-doubt in relation to competence, a sense of collegial disapproval, and isolation (Boice, 1993).

Similarly, due to lack of procedural employment protections, administrators can receive little advance warning of impending, negative employment actions. Recall the abruptness of the lunch-hour firings at Auburn University in 2004 when email privileges were revoked before the administrators could return to their offices. Recall also how Claudia, the African American female administrator was escorted off campus by security without warning in an undignified manner and how an investigation of Julie, a white female administrator, was undertaken without advance notice. The compounding of indignities in these cases is further support for the analogy of administrative working conditions to a form of indentured servitude. Returning to the study of 996 recently laid-off or fired employees in Ohio cited earlier, the magnitude of unfair treatment that "adds the insult of undignified treatment to the injury of job loss" heightens the potential for litigation (Lind, Greenberg, Scott, and Welchans, 2000, p. 585). The researchers in this study concluded that terminated employees need to maintain a positive self-identity when the relationship to the employer is removed as well as traditional assistance and honest accounts to ease the psychological shock of job loss (Lind, Greenberg, Scott, and Welchans, 2000).

What then can diverse administrators do to avoid such precarious employment conditions? In the next section, we discuss factors that will help diverse administrators evaluate job opportunities and identify welcoming work environments that will support their career success.

Aligning Expectations with Reality

As diverse individuals enter the administrative track or are offered job opportunities at other institutions, gauging the climate of the new work environment is particularly critical in terms of determining how their contributions will be received. Several considerations in addition to the level of responsibility, salary, and geographic location may help determine whether a career move is optimal and whether a new work environment will offer greater internal support, career growth, and job satisfaction.

Job Security

The most significant issue facing diverse administrators is job security, given the potential for subtle discrimination and the lack of legal redress once situations of subtle discrimination arise. Clearly, the greatest point of leverage for administrators is at the time of the job offer when employment terms are negotiated. The offer letter and employment contract, if a contract is provided, are pivotal documents that codify the results of the negotiating process. These documents usually indicate that administrators serve in at will status and "at the pleasure of" the supervisor. Before accepting an offer, administrators need to review the institution's policies for non-renewal, including the notice period given. Although applicants may feel pressure to accept the terms as offered based upon economic need or the appeal of a higher salary, no more critical opportunity exists for creating more stable employment conditions than at the time of job offer. Negotiating for tenure rights, retreat rights, sabbaticals, or multi-year options may not always be feasible, but any stronger guarantee of stability will help ensure a successful experience and greater employment longevity.

Diversity Climate and Executive Turnover

An institution's track record with respect to diversity, including level of turnover as well as rate of internal promotion for minority and female executive leaders, can also provide some indication of the level of support for diversity. Clues to administrative climate can be obtained during the interview process, including informal statements by other administrators, the types of questions asked by search committee members or employees in open forums, the interactions among executive staff, and the level of reciprocal interaction in the supervisory interview.

In terms of organizational stability, one of the issues raised by a number of the interviewees is the relatively common phenomenon of turnover of supervisors, resulting in less favorable treatment of diverse administrators by a subsequent supervisor. For example, Mark, the Asian American administrator cited earlier, described how a high-ranking mid-level minority administrator came under the supervision of a new white vice president, and within a short period of time, a number of disagreements arose. The vice president took disciplinary steps that the administrator found degrading, resulting in her early separation as well as a great deal of personal suffering on her part. We have also seen in the first-hand accounts of Michael, a black male administrator, and Christine, a white female LGBT administrator, the impact of a change in supervision in how they were treated. As a result, when evaluating potential working conditions in a new administrative environment, the relative stability of supervision can also be an issue for consideration.

Countervailing Forces and Executive Sponsorship

Frequently high-level executive sponsors chair administrative search committees and board members or other executive team members may participate in the search process. Such individuals may serve as informal sponsors or mentors for diverse administrators, having a vested interest in the success of the candidate due to their involvement in the search process. The potential for such mentorship and stabilizing alliances is a critical consideration in the evaluation of job opportunities.

Micro-climates

The climate for diversity varies considerably within different divisions and departments, given the decentralized context of the university. As Jon, the white male academic administrator cited earlier notes:

> It's not universal, and I think some departments have problems in that area, and some don't. And I think that's true of the university in general. That's a constant message from the upper administration to try to get women and people of color into leadership positions. But the day-to-day life in many of our departments where you have a faculty or senior leadership that doesn't think that there is a problem, or for political or ideological reasons, that's where we have the problems.

Evaluation of a particular department's climate may be difficult to outsiders, but indicators include the level of structural representation, the observed climate or atmosphere on a walk-through, and informal observations and cues shared during the interview process. When individuals have the ability to make choices in an administrative assignment, the factors identified here may help provide insight into the level of support for diversity in a particular environment. The decision-making process can be supplemented by a review of institutional policies, discussions with key individuals, and interactions during the interview process.

Concluding Perspectives

In this chapter, we have identified promising practices at a number of research universities that represent forward-looking and sustainable solutions to building a strong administrative talent base that will support the evolutionary aims of world-class institutions in a global society. Institutional resilience requires re-examination of the principles and practices of shared governance to counteract atrophying trends that splinter the university's democratic mission and purposes. And diverse talent and shared governance are at the core of the process of institutional reinvention. Even benign neglect of how the forces of power and diversity intersect on a daily basis in administrative leadership is a course detrimental to the university's pursuit of integrity and effectiveness.

As a result, the process of systemic organizational change needs to draw upon the tools developed by leading researchers to understand the collision between systems of power and the experiences of diverse individuals in the higher education workplace. The rich legacy of research, particularly through the writing of women, minority, and LGBT faculty, has documented the ways in which subtle discrimination permeates the academic arena. The concrete diversity strategic action plans cited in this chapter provide an uncompromising mandate for institutional transformation in support of diversity and inclusion. Concerted, collective action by administrators, faculty, and staff will be needed to galvanize support for diversity action that affects the administrative tier. New leadership models will benefit from consideration of prevailing internal barriers to survival and success faced by diverse leaders.

In this regard, a report issued by the Leadership Community in a collaborative research initiative on "Leadership for a New Era" suggests that leadership programs that focus only upon equal opportunity and diversity practices do not address the interplay of culture, institutional policies, and career and life opportunities for disadvantaged groups (Chun, 2010; Keleher et al., 2010). In fact, the report found almost 90 percent of the 122 institutional leadership programs surveyed address diversity, but only half include training on structural racism and white privilege (Chun, 2010; Keleher et al., 2010). Discussion of the systems that perpetuate social stratification—racism, sexism, heterosexism, classism, ableism, and other forms of exclusion—is still seen as controversial within the context of existing leadership programs.

One of the most promising initiatives to promote serious dialogue around sensitive diversity issues has been the Ford Foundation's "Difficult Dialogues Initiative" (DDI) launched in 2005. Twenty-seven higher education institutions were selected from 675 preliminary proposals and awarded grants of $100,000 to develop projects that promote campus environments where sensitive subjects could be discussed in support of a spirit of open scholarly inquiry, academic freedom, and diverse viewpoints. For example, the University of Missouri received $200,000 in grant funding in 2005 and 2008 to develop the phases of a program designed to teach and reinforce knowledge, skills, and awareness of diversity issues relating to race, gender, sexual orientation, and religious literacy needed for democratic participation in a global society ("Promoting Pluralism," 2009). A summer institute designed to help other institutions develop DDI programs on their own campuses was designed by program leaders at the University of Missouri, the University of Texas at Austin and the University of Alaska, Anchorage ("Making a Difference Through Dialogue," 2009). Earlier in the book, we have also mentioned the Intergroup Dialogue Program developed at the University of Michigan as a leading program based upon the core principle of social justice that has been implemented at a significant number of research universities.

As the landscape for higher education has shifted dramatically in light of budgetary constraints and resource limitations, reform and reconceptualization of leadership practices in the research university has attained new urgency. In his 2010 State of the University Address, University of Minnesota's President Robert H. Bruininks called for a culture of renewal and a renaissance in higher education, noting that "at best, great universities are pioneering, savvy, and inspired; at their worst, they cling to their medieval roots" when turned to the past (Bruininks, 2010). In turning away from past hierarchical practices that sustain patterns of social stratification, universities are poised to create a new infrastructure of inclusion that will support the creativity, talent, and innovative contributions of a diverse administrative leadership. Strong and positive steps must be taken to strengthen the representation of diverse administrators, build durable accountability structures, eliminate ascriptive inequality in organizational processes, and create stable administrative employment conditions.

Works Cited

100 commitments. (2010). Retrieved December 22, 2010, from Kent State University Web site: http://www.kent.edu/diversity/100commitments/index.cfm.

4.7 sabbatical leaves. (1999). Retrieved November 28, 2010, from Minnesota State Colleges and Universities Web site: http://www.mnscu.edu/board/policy/407.html.

Administrative fellows program. (2008). Retrieved December 10, 2010, from Illinois State University, Faculty and Staff Web site: http://www.cas.ilstu.edu/faculty/request.shtm.

Administrative fellows program. (2010). Retrieved December 10, 2010, from Penn State, Office of the Vice Provost for Academic Affairs Web site: http://www.psu.edu/dept/vprov/adminfellows.htm.

Anderson, J. A. (2008). *Driving change through diversity and globalization: Transformative leadership in the academy.* Sterling, VA: Stylus.

Birnbaum, R. (2004, Fall). The end of shared governance: Looking ahead or looking back. *New Directions For Higher Education,* 127, 5–22.

Boice, R. (1993). Early turning points in professorial careers of women and minorities. *New Directions for Teaching and Learning,* 53, 71–79.

Bruininks, R. H. (2010). *Chartering the future: Community leadership during transition: 2010 State of the university address.* Retrieved December 22, 2010, from http://blog.lib .umn.edu /pres/news/2010%20State%20of%20the%20University%20Address.pdf.

Chun, E. (2010). *Do subtle discrimination and social justice belong in leadership development programs?* Retrieved December 22, 2010, from http://www.racismreview.com/blog/ author/ednac/.

Cross, W. E. (1971). The negro to black conversion experience: Towards a psychology of black liberation. *Black World,* 20(9), 13–27.

Cross, W. E. (1978). The Thomas and Cross models of psychological nigrescence: A review. *Journal of Black Psychology,* 5(1), 13–31.

Eckel, P. D., and Kezar, A. (2003). *Taking the reins: Institutional transformation in higher education.* Westport, CT: Praeger Publishers.

Ely, R. F., and Rhode, D. L. (2010). Women and leadership: Defining the challenges. In N. Nohria and R. Khurana (Eds.), *Handbook of leadership theory and practice* (pp. 377–410). Boston: Harvard Business School.

Examples of appointments for full-time non tenure track faculty at selected institutions. (n.d.). Retrieved November 14, 2010, from http://www.rutgersaaup.org/misc/ntt%20 research%20on%20appointments.pdf.

Exempt & non-exempt staff: Affinity groups. (n.d.). Retrieved December 29, 2010, from Syracuse University, Human Resources Web site: http://humanresources.syr.edu/ staff/nbu_staff/affinity.html.

Feagin, J. R. (2010). *The white racial frame: Centuries of racial framing and counter-framing.* New York: Routledge.

A framework to foster diversity at Penn State 2010–15. (n.d.). Retrieved December 3, 2010, from Penn State Web site: http://www.equity.psu.edu/framework/pdf/ framework_2010_15.pdf.

Gee, G. (2009). Foreword. In J. C. Knapp and D. J. Siegel (Eds.), *The business of higher education: Volume 1: Leadership and culture* (pp. vii–x). Santa Barbara, CA: Praeger Perspectives.

Goins, G. J. (2010, December). Leveraging affinity groups in tough economic times: Practical steps to demonstrate value. *INSIGHT into Diversity,* 32–33.

Grievance procedure for administrators. (2005). Retrieved November 28, 2010, from Southern Oregon University Web site: http://sou.edu/policies/Grievances-admin.pdf.

Harvard Medical School and Harvard School of Dental Medicine procedures for resolving complaints of discrimination, harassment, or unprofessional relationships and abuse of authority. (2008). Retrieved December 10, 2010, from Harvard Medical School, Ombuds Office Web site: http://www.hms.harvard.edu/ombuds/complain.html.

Hockfield, S. (2010). *Letters to the community: Statement on the report on the initiative for faculty race and diversity.* Retrieved November 28, 2010, from http://web.mit.edu/ hockfield /letters/ letter01142010.html.

Ibarra, H. (1999). Provisional selves: Experimenting with image and identity in professional adaptation. *Administrative Science Quarterly,* 44(4), 764–791.

Ibarra, H., Snook, S., and Ramo, L. G. (2010). Identity-based leader development. In N. Nohria and R. Khurana (Eds.), *Handbook of leadership theory and practice* (pp. 657–679). Boston: Harvard Business School.

Jordan-Zachery, J. S. (2004). Reflections on mentoring: Black women and the academy. *PS: Political Science and Politics,* 37(4), 875–877.

Keleher, T., Leiderman, S., Meehan, D., Perry, E., Potapchuk, M., Powell, J. A., et al. (2010). *Leadership & race: How to develop and support leadership that contributes to racial justice.* Retrieved December 22, 2010, from http://leadershiplearning.org/system/files/ Leadership%20and%20Race%20FINAL_Electronic_072010.pdf.

Kezar, A. (2004, Fall). What is more important to effective governance: Relationships, trust, and leadership, or structures and formal processes? *New Directions for Higher Education,* 127, 35–46.

Kezar, A. (2010). Rethinking postsecondary institutions for low-income student success: The power of post-structural theory. In A. Kezar (Ed.), *Recognizing and serving low-income students in higher education: An examination of institutional policies, practices and culture* (pp. 3–26). New York: Routledge.

Kezar, A., and Carducci, R. (2009). Revolutionizing leadership development: Lessons from research and theory. In A. Kezar (Ed.), *Rethinking leadership in a complex, multicultural, and global environment: New concepts and models for higher education* (pp. 1–38). Sterling, VA: Stylus.

Kezar, A., Lester, J., and Anderson, G. (2006, Fall). Challenging stereotypes that interfere with effective governance. *The NEA Higher Education Journal,* 121–134.

Leymann, H. (1990). Mobbing and psychological terror at workplaces. *Violence and Victims,* 5(2), 119–126.

Lind, E. A., Greenberg, J., Scott, K. S., and Welchans, T. D. (2000). The winding road from employee to complainant: Situational and psychological determinants of wrongful-termination claims. *Administrative Science Quarterly,* 45(3), 557–590.

Lord, R. G., and Hall, R. J. (2005). Identity, deep structure and the development of leadership skill. *The Leadership Quarterly,* 16(4), 591–615.

Making a difference through dialogue: About the institute. (2009). Retrieved December 22, 2010, from University of Missouri, Difficult Dialogues Web site: http:// difficultdialogues.missouri.edu/summer-institute/index.php.

Marginson, S. (2004). Going global: Governance implications of cross-border traffic in higher education. In W. G. Tierney (Ed.), *Competing conceptions of academic governance: Negotiating the perfect storm* (pp. 1–32). Baltimore: Johns Hopkins University Press.

Mayhew, M. J., and Engberg, M. E. (2010). Diversity and moral reasoning: How negative diverse peer interactions affect the development of moral reasoning in undergraduate students. *The Journal of Higher Education,* 81(4), 459–488.

Minnesota state colleges & universities: Personnel plan for administrators: 7/1/2009–6/30/2011. (2009). Retrieved November 28, 2010, from Minnesota State Colleges and Universities

Web site: http://www.hr.mnscu.edu/contract_plans/documents/ AdminPlan10_11_2 .pdf.

Mission. (n.d.). Retrieved December 10, 2010, from Massachusetts Institute of Technology, Ombuds Office Web site: http://web.mit.edu/ombud/index.html.

Paige, R. M. (2005). *Internationalization of higher education: Performance assessment and indicators.* Retrieved December 28, 2010, from http://www.cshe.nagoya-u.ac.jp/ publications/journal/no5/08.pdf.

Policy 6-314: Leaves of absence (effective fall semester 1998). (1997). Retrieved November 28, 2010, from The University of Utah, Regulations Library Web site: http://www .regulations.utah.edu/academics/6-314.html.

The principles of community. (n.d.). Retrieved November 18, 2010, from UC Davis Web site: http://principles.ucdavis.edu/default.html.

Principles of community reaffirmed. (2010). Retrieved November 18, 2010, from UC Davis Web site: http://principles.ucdavis.edu/Content/PDF/PrinciplesofCommunity2010 .pdf.

Professional coaching: Understand. (2007). Retrieved December 10, 2010, from University of Washington, Professional & Organizational Development: A Division of Human Resources Web site: http://www.washington.edu/admin/hr/pod/coaching/index.html.

Promoting pluralism and academic freedom on campus: Welcome. (2009). Retrieved December 22, 2010, from University of Missouri, Difficult Dialogues Web site: http:// difficultdialogues.missouri.edu/.

Ragins, B. R. (1997). Diversified mentoring relationships in organizations: A power perspective. *The Academy of Management Review, 22*(2), 482–521.

Ragins, B. R., and Cotton, J. L. (1999). Mentor functions and outcomes: A comparison of men and women in formal and informal mentoring relationships. *Journal of Applied Psychology, 84*(4), 529–550.

Ragins, B. R., and Sundstrom, E. (1989). Gender and power in organizations: A longitudinal perspective. *Psychological Bulletin, 105*(1), 51–88.

Rhoades, G. (1983). Conflicting interests in higher education. *American Journal of Education, 91*(3), 283–327.

Rowe, M. P. (1993). Options and choice for conflict resolution in the workplace. In L. Hall (Ed.), *Negotiation: Strategies for mutual gain: The basic seminar of the program on negotiation at Harvard Law School* (pp. 105–120). Thousand Oaks, CA: Sage Publications.

Rowe, M. P. (1996). Dealing with harassment: A systems approach. In M. S. Stockdale (Ed.), *Sexual harassment in the workplace: Perspectives, frontiers, and response strategies: Women and work series, Vol. 5* (pp. 241–271). Thousand Oaks, CA: Sage Publications.

Salmi, J. (2009). *The challenge of establishing world class universities.* Washington, DC: The World Bank.

Senior administrative fellows program. (2010). Retrieved December 10, 2010, from The University of Kansas, Office of the Provost Web site: http://www.provost.ku.edu/ areas/faculty/development/senioradminfellows.shtml.

Senior management group performance management review process. (2010). Retrieved December 10, 2010, from The University of California Web site: http://www .universityofcalifornia.edu/regents/policies/7702.pdf.

Siegel, D. J. (2003). *The call for diversity: Pressure, expectation and organizational response in the post secondary setting.* New York: Routledge Falmer.

Siegel, D. J. (2009). Changing the subject: Collective action as a new form of "corporate" influence. In J. C. Knapp and D. J. Siegel (Eds.), *The business of higher education: Volume 1: Leadership and culture* (pp. 31–52). Santa Barbara, CA: Praeger Perspectives.

Siegel, D. J. (2010). *Organizing for social partnership: Higher education in cross-sector collaboration.* New York: Routledge.

Slaughter, S., and Rhoades, G. (2004). *Academic capitalism and the new economy: Markets, state, and higher education.* Baltimore: Johns Hopkins University Press.

Strathe, M. I., and Wilson, V. W. (2006). *In their own words: Mentoring in the changing academy: Attending to context—Part 1.* Retrieved December 20, 2010, from Women in Higher Education Web site: http://www.wihe.com/displayNews.jsp?id=397.

Tatum, B. D. (1997). *"Why are all the black kids sitting together in the cafeteria?": A psychologist explains the development of racial identity.* New York: Basic Books.

Texas A&M University diversity plan: Accountability, climate, equity. (n.d.). Retrieved December 20, 2010, from Texas A&M University, Office of the Vice President and Associate Provost for Diversity Web site: http://diversity.tamu.edu/Documents/DiversityPlan.pdf.

Thomas, D. A. (1990). The impact of race on managers' experiences of developmental relationships (mentoring and sponsorship): An intra-organizational study. *Journal of Organizational Behavior,* 11(6), 479–492.

Tierney, W. G. (2004). Introduction: A perfect storm: Turbulence in higher education. In W. G. Tierney (Ed.), *Competing conceptions of academic governance: Negotiating the perfect storm* (pp. 1–32). Baltimore: Johns Hopkins University Press.

Toma, J. D. (2010). *Building organizational capacity: Strategic management in higher education.* Baltimore: Johns Hopkins University Press.

Trow, M. (1998). On the accountability of higher education in the United States. In W. G. Bowen and H. T. Shapiro (Eds.), *Universities and their leadership* (pp. 15–64). Princeton, NJ: Princeton University Press.

The Trustees of Princeton University. (2010). *Rights, rules, responsibilities.* Retrieved November 18, 2010, from Princeton University Web site: http://www.princeton.edu/pub/rrr/part1/.

Women supporting women's mission. (n.d.). Retrieved December 10, 2010, from Carnegie Mellon, Human Resources Web site: http://www.cmu.edu/hr/learning/professional/wsw.html.

Zellers, D. F., Howard, V. M., and Barcic, M. A. (2008). Faculty mentoring programs: Reenvisioning rather than reinventing the wheel. *Review of Educational Research,* 78(3), 552–588.

5

SUMMARY AND RECOMMENDATIONS FOR INSTITUTIONAL CHANGE

> We don't control things we should control..... It's a guessing game. I don't have much say in my own budget; hiring, very limited in determining what the level of the position should be; serving on committees, there are some committees that my position should represent, I don't even know if I will get an opportunity to be there; nor am I participating in the discussions that would make that decision.... To have people make good decisions, you have to be at the table talking with them. I'm not doing that.
>
> —*Lisa, an African American administrator*

Lisa's account of her limited job authority, lack of participation in decision making, and lack of support in her campuswide role, powerfully illustrates the mechanisms of exclusion in the university workplace. As the first in-depth study of the experiences of minority, female, and LGBT administrators in higher education, this book has examined the complex interplay of power and privilege and the intensification of inequality at higher levels of the university. Understanding racism, sexism, and heterosexism as a system of advantage is antithetical to American notions of meritocracy (Tatum, 1997). And yet we have seen how systems of social stratification are reproduced within the norms, practices, and day-to-day interactions of the university workplace and identified the persistence of deeply rooted, process-based patterns of subtle discrimination that exact a high personal and professional cost upon diverse administrators.

The methodology of the study draws upon the hermeneutic dimension of participant observation to explore how everyday experiences of diverse administrative leaders illuminate larger patterns of social exclusion. The survey findings have documented experiences of mistreatment, subtle discrimination, and lack of positional authority reported by diverse administrators. As a result, the analogy of indentured servitude portrays the heightened vulnerability of minority, women, and LGBT administrators who typically function in at will employment relationships without security or stability.

Through the interviews, we have seen significant commonalities in *how* discriminatory practices unfold in the research university, regardless of geographic location, institutional prestige, or the public/private status of the institution. The striking similarity in the processes of subtle discrimination validates the emergence of a new and toxic taxonomy of micro-aggressions and micro-inequities that has emerged in a post-civil rights era.

Perhaps some may be surprised or even shocked to read the first-hand accounts of both covert and overt discrimination of diverse administrators. We have seen how terms such as "Oreo" and "Africa girl" were used by supervisors in public settings. Both Claudia and Michael related statements made to them indicating that they represent exceptions to their race as African American administrators. Diverse administrators experience considerable isolation, and may personalize their situations and engage in self-blame, unaware of the commonality of their experiences across institutional settings. And as Mark and Lisa indicated, they also are subject to continual anxiety and ambiguity in their environments, feeling around for clues and having to wonder in advance about what to do or say, due to the perceived lack of acceptance of their leadership role.

Due to the exclusivity of the at will employment relationship at higher administrative levels, executive gatekeepers retain relatively singular control of the processes of compensation, evaluation, promotion, advancement, and termination for administrators. Structural and contextual factors provide the medium through which inequality is reproduced, without the benefit of employment protections, institutional interference, or legal remedies. Furthermore, white gatekeepers may differ significantly in their frontstage and backstage presences: a certain performativity characterizes how they present themselves as "color-blind" on the front stage, while backstage comments, emotions, and actions reveal racist, sexist, and heterosexist views (Picca and Feagin, 2007). The collusion of bystanders contributes to these performances either through active participation or passive non-interference in the competitive effort to gain power and the fear of repercussions from powerful supervisors.

The cloak of meritocratic justification provides the rationale for formal acts of social closure. Fuzzy, indeterminate, and subjective criteria based upon soft skills such as teamwork, collegial interactions, collaboration, and ability to fit in can be used to cast doubt on the personal competency and effectiveness of diverse administrators. And asymmetrical power relationships may also create the potential for systematic mistreatment and psychological terrorization through bullying, veiled threats, and continuous psychological abuse as forms of manipulation that further isolate and ostracize diverse individuals. Significant research findings link the "minority stress model" caused by multiple disadvantaged social categories such as race, gender, and sexual orientation to increased vulnerability to stress and compromised health outcomes.

Given the pressures of globalization, diminishing budgets, and increased public accountability, the university's mission in the advancement and creation of knowledge relies more than ever upon the ability to mobilize the strength of a diverse talent base. The high cost to the university of excluding and wasting the vast resources of knowledge, creativity, and innovation of diverse administrative talent threatens institutional integrity and cohesion. In addition, practices of everyday oppression in the leadership ranks undermine the university's moral and social leadership and its democratic educational purposes. Just as Abraham Lincoln identified the perils of a house divided against itself in his June 16, 1858 speech to the Republican convention, the university's survival is dependent upon resolving its internal contradictions— and in Lincoln's words to "become all one thing or all the other" ("House Divided Speech," 1958, para. 12).

Recent research discussed in the study identifies the importance of a reconceptualized leadership model that replaces coercive, top-down management practices with revolutionary models based upon collaboration, empowerment, and inclusiveness. Several promising trends suggest the potential for a different administrative future built upon the foundations of Inclusive Excellence. The growing awareness among tenured faculty of the dangers of corporatization within the academy provides the opportunity for collective action to unite the university's disparate employment realities.

Looking Forward

We have shared examples of presidents of major research institutions who envision the reinvention of the university in light of present challenges and future opportunities. Perhaps the time has come to reinvent leadership and to think differently about how universities are managed. For this reason, the emerging concept of *intergroup leadership* builds common ground when fused with principles of shared governance in the research university. The future of shared governance will depend upon the academy's ability to reendow governance as a common vehicle that promotes collaboration through intergroup leadership rather than intergroup rivalry (Crellin, 2010). Effective intergroup leadership mobilizes and motivates groups to work productively with those initially seen as different (Kanter, 2009). Intergroup leadership overcomes the fragmentation of in-groups and out-groups whose enmity is perpetuated through hoarding, passivity, and defensiveness, requiring needless resource expenditure on policing boundaries (Kanter, 2009).

And intergroup leadership offers the potential for *boundaryless leadership* that bridges social identity groups in service of a larger organizational vision (Ernst and Yip, 2009). The process of decategorization that emerges from boundaryless leadership creates a third space, a neutral zone, with emphasis on individuals, rather than social categories (Ernst and Yip, 2009).

From the perspective of diverse administrators, we have indicated the value of building a collective consciousness as a buffer for discrimination. Too often identity groups perceive themselves as separate and do not join in the powerful alliances needed to bring about change. As part of this process, development of critical counter frames of resistance will help defuse existing racist, sexist, and heterosexist frames. The repertoire of strategies shared by administrators in this study includes naming discrimination *in the moment* it occurs—interrupting the flow of discriminatory statements or acts whenever possible. In addition, problem-focused coping or emotion-focused strategies can help diverse administrators minimize the impact of discriminatory situations and preserve self-esteem through anticipation, cognitive restructuring, and emotional control.

In light of the need for concrete liberation strategies that operationalize academic freedom within the administrative context, we have proposed a range of concrete solutions based upon best practices in the research university today. As a result, we summarize our recommendations for a forward-looking agenda for administrators into three categories: structural, procedural, and behavioral.

Structural Recommendations

- Increase representational diversity by hiring women, minority, and LGBT administrators in positions of line authority, including executive positions traditionally held by white males.

- Vest diverse administrators with appropriate authority and resources commensurate with the level of their position and ensure comparability in similar level positions.
- Systematically compare resource allocations for comparable administrator positions as gauged by funding; number of reclassifications; number of lines allocated; compensation awards; promotions; and other internal opportunities.
- Monitor employment patterns by organizational area and supervisory purview for hiring, promotion, compensation, evaluation, and termination decisions in terms of adverse impact upon diverse administrators. Review supervisory-subordinate demography as an essential variable in this analysis.
- Implement due process protections in employment processes affecting administrators.
- Establish multi-year contracts for administrators.
- Implement an integrated Conflict Management system.

Procedural Recommendations

- Eliminate "wired searches" or waivers and strengthen diversity recruitment; ensure diversity of search committees.
- Provide multiple points of review for all employment decisions.
- Ensure objectivity of administrative evaluation systems through goal setting and resultant accomplishments.
- Establish diversity criteria for administrative evaluations and reward substantive diversity contributions.
- Evaluate distribution of professional development opportunities for comparable level positions in terms of potential ascriptive inequality.
- Provide administrator sabbaticals and other professional development opportunities.
- Create an administrator manual that identifies relevant resources, policies, and support structures that can help diverse administrators successfully navigate the organization.
- Promote organizational learning directed toward raising awareness relating to subtle discrimination, micro-inequities, and social justice issues.
- Create safety zones or safe spaces and identify institutional allies.
- Partner with interested stakeholders in forming affinity groups and provide executive sponsorship.

Behavioral Recommendations

- Monitor campus climate and micro-climates through a climate study that includes administrators.
- Sponsor difficult dialogues or the Intergroup Dialogue Program to jump start discussions of sensitive issues relating to diversity.
- Provide diverse administrators with opportunities to interact both formally and informally with other university executives, members of the board of trustees, and prominent community members.
- Establish informal and formal mentoring programs that provide coaching opportunities.
- Encourage regular, informal supervisory-subordinate interactions and listening opportunities.
- Encourage continuous coaching and feedback based upon identified goals and objectives.

Finally, the elimination of unfairness, mistreatment, marginalization, and discrimination in the administrative workplace is essential to the development of inclusive and ethical leadership practices. Recognition and celebration of the talents of all members of the university community will strengthen the creation of a climate of respect, dignity, and empowerment that supports the attainment of Inclusive Excellence.

Just as we opened the book with Claudia's description of her mistreatment by her supervisor, we conclude now with her vision for a different future:

> I hope that I live to see the end of discrimination, all forms of discrimination for all people. We are all people. We are all flesh-and-blood human beings. We all have a right to be here. We all have a right to reach our fullest potential. And I think as fellow human beings we have a responsibility to one other to help our other fellow human beings to reach their goals, to reach their fullest potential. . . . Certainly the person has to take that leap. But if I was a little bit of wind beneath their wings, then I think that is what I was supposed to do. I think that when I die and meet my maker, he will say, you know what, you did what I sent you down there to do. That's the way I think we all want to be treating each other . . . and accepting each other for our uniqueness and diversity and the great qualities and the things that we each can contribute to this life.

Works Cited

Crellin, M. A. (2010, Fall). The future of shared governance. *New Directions for Higher Education, 151*, 71–81.

Ernst, C., and Yip, J. (2009). Boundary-spanning leadership: Tactics to bridge social identity groups in organizations. In T. L. Pittinsky (Ed.), *Crossing the divide: Intergroup leadership in a world of difference* (pp. 73–86). Boston: Harvard Business School Publishing.

House divided speech: Springfield, Illinois: June 16, 1858. (1958). Retrieved December 30, 2010, from http://showcase.netins.net/web/creative/lincoln/speeches/house.htm.

Kanter, R. M. (2009). Creating common ground: Propositions about effective intergroup leadership. In T. L. Pittinsky (Ed.), *Crossing the divide: Intergroup leadership in a world of difference* (pp. 73–86). Boston: Harvard Business School Publishing.

Picca, L. H., and Feagin, J. (2007). *Two-faced racism: Whites in the backstage and frontstage.* New York: Routledge.

Tatum, B. D. (1997). *"Why are all the black kids sitting together in the cafeteria?": A psychologist explains the development of racial identity.* New York: Basic Books.

APPENDIX A

Methodology for the Study

This study examined the following four research questions:

1. In what ways do female, minority, and LGBT administrators experience subtle, covert, and even overt discrimination in their work environments in higher education? Do they experience a lack of support from their supervisors? Do they experience isolation and tokenism, marginalization, lack of empowerment, differential expectations, bullying, and psychological abuse?
2. What barriers do diverse administrators experience in terms of formal, organizational processes such as performance evaluation, promotion, and compensation compared to their counterparts?
3. Do female, minority, and LGBT administrators experience significant and sustained stress due to subtle discrimination and lack of stability and support in their roles? What mental and physical impact do behavioral and organizational barriers have upon minority and female administrators?
4. What specific strategies and approaches have helped diverse administrators resist and overcome the discriminatory barriers they encounter?

To explore these questions as an intensive case study of American leadership and the collision between everyday life and systems of power, we conducted a written survey using a representative sample of administrators in research universities throughout the United States and conducted follow-up telephone interviews. The following email was sent to 300 higher-education administrators in public and private research universities, using an initial contact database of Chief Human Resource Officers:

Dear [Name]:

As a higher-education colleague, we are writing to request your assistance on an important research project that seeks to gather data on barriers to inclusion for minority, female, and LGBT administrators at the level of Director and up at research universities. We are seeking participants to complete a short six-minute survey and planning to summarize this research in an upcoming publication.

By way of background, we have recently published two books—*Bridging the Diversity Divide: Globalization and Reciprocal Empowerment in Higher Education* (Jossey Bass, 2009) and *Are the Walls Really Down? Behavioral and Organizational Barriers to Faculty and Staff Diversity* (Jossey Bass, 2007)—that examine behavioral and organizational barriers to diversity at public research universities from a practitioner's perspective.

For the administrator research survey, we seek both minority and majority, and male and female participants at the level of Director and up to validate the sample. We would like to ask if you would be willing to participate and also to share this invitation with several colleagues who are administrators at your university to participate. We would appreciate it if you could include minority and female administrators in this invitation.

The survey is password protected and on a Web site entitled adminsurvey.com. The password for the survey is xxxx. All data is strictly confidential and no individual information including name, title, institution, or personal data, will be connected with the individual completing the survey. We also will invite participants to participate in a confidential followup phone or in-person interview to obtain more in-depth information.

Should you have any questions, we can be reached at xxx-xxx-xxxx or by email. Thank you so much for your willingness to participate.

Sincerely,
Edna Chun and Alvin Evans

APPENDIX B

Data Sample

Written Survey Sample

Forty-three administrators in public and private research universities completed the contact information and answered most or all of the questions in an online written survey. The demographics of the written survey participants included thirty-five females and eight males, with thirteen African Americans, twenty-six whites, one Asian, two other or two-or-more races, and one not identified. In addition, six individuals are Hispanic in ethnicity. Of the sample, three individuals self-identified as homosexual/gay.

The survey sample reflected all geographic areas with eleven individuals from institutions in the East, nine in the Midwest, twelve in the South, two in the Southwest, six in the West, and three unidentified. Position titles of participants are at the level of director and up, including twenty-three directors, two executive directors, six vice presidents or provosts, two chief diversity officers or diversity officers, five assistant/associate vice chancellors, two associate deans/executive associate deans, one registrar, and two without a title indicated.

Since the initial contact was made with Chief Human Resource officers in most instances, the sample contains a large number of human resource professionals. The fields represented in the sample included six in Affirmative Action, four in Diversity, seven in Academic Affairs, two in Finance, two in Student Affairs, seventeen in Human Resources, two in Human Resources and Diversity, one in Information Technology, one in Advancement, and one in multiple areas. The sample included eighteen individuals with doctorates as the highest degree, nineteen with master's degrees, and six with bachelor's degrees.

Interview Sample

Of the forty-three administrators responding to the written survey, twenty-four administrators indicated a willingness to be interviewed. Due to the fact that one administrator had already left her position and two did not respond to the interview request, twenty-one administrators were interviewed. The interview sample was diverse and included five males and sixteen females as well as five African Americans, one Asian American, and fifteen whites. In terms of ethnicity, three participants self-identified as Hispanic. In addition, the interview sample included two participants who self-identified as homosexual/gay. The interview participants work in public and private research universities in all geographic regions: six in the East, six in the South, four in the Midwest, two in the Southwest, and three in the West.

The interviews were conducted over the telephone, and each interview lasted one hour. Before each interview, informed consent was obtained to record the interview and the participants were provided with the transcribed passages selected for publication for their review and consent. The interviews used four vignettes adapted from scenarios in the research literature to elicit interviewee feedback, followed by a number of open-ended questions.

INDEX

Note: Page numbers followed by *t* indicate tables.

Tenure, protection of, 17
Texas A&M University, 120–121
Thomas, Roosevelt, 43
Threats, veiled, 130–131
Title VII, Civil Rights Act (1964), 24, 25
Tokenism theory, 11
Total institution concept, 74, 98
Transformation of administrative
    culture: exemplary practices and
    strategies, 117–127; need for,
    111–113, 143; overview of, 134–136;
    recommendations for, 143–146;
    reconceptualized leadership model,
    113–117, 143
Transgendered individuals: hate crimes
    against, 9; stress and, 55
Traumatic assault, 56–57
Turning points, rapid and irreversible,
    131–132
Turnover of supervisors, 133

Unconscious bias, 24
Unintentional intolerance, forms of, 22
University of Alaska, Anchorage, 136
University of California at Davis, 119
University of California System, 123
University of Chicago, 80
University of Kansas, 126
University of Maryland, 14
University of Michigan, 60, 136
University of Minnesota, 136
University of Missouri, 135–136
University of Northern Iowa, 4
University of Texas at Austin, 136
University of Utah, 124
University of Vermont, 3

University of Washington, 126
Usurpation, definition of, 2

Variables of investigation, 8–10
Victim-perpetrator-guardian model, 51, 53

"Warm" emotional systems, 58
Warning signs of non-welcoming
    environments: bullying and veiled
    threats, 130–131; distortion and
    stereotypes regarding attributes of
    power, 128–129; invisibility and
    exclusion, 129–130; lack of coaching,
    131; magnification of mistakes, 131;
    rapid, irreversible turning points,
    131–132; restricted authority and
    resources, 127–128
Weber, Max, 41
Whistleblower Enhancement Act (2007),
    25
White privilege, 1, 18
White racial frame, 38
Wiring of candidate searches, 87, 88
Women: ethgender discrimination and,
    17; in university administration,
    10–11
Work environment: climate of
    organizational justice in, 25–26;
    dynamics of power in, 19, 39; impact
    of social stigma in, 45–50; intersection
    of dynamic process of discrimination
    with, 39–45; victim-perpetrator-
    guardian model in, 51. *See also*
    Inequality in workplace; Warning
    signs of non-welcoming environments
Wu, Frank, 60

ABOUT THE AUTHORS

Edna Chun is Associate Vice Chancellor for Human Resource Services at the University of North Carolina at Greensboro. Alvin Evans serves as Associate Vice President for Kent State University. Their two earlier books, *Are the Walls Really Down? Behavioral and Organizational Barriers to Faculty and Staff Diversity* (2007) and *Bridging the Diversity Divide: Globalization and Reciprocal Empowerment in Higher Education* (2009), were both recipients of the prestigious Kathryn G. Hanson Publication Award by the national College and University Professional Association for Human Resources.